Understanding the Human Mind

The Danger of Negative Thinking

Jason Browne

© Copyright 2021 - All rights reserved.

The content contained within this book may not be reproduced, duplicated or transmitted without direct written permission from the author or the publisher.

Under no circumstances will any blame or legal responsibility be held against the publisher, or author, for any damages, reparation, or monetary loss due to the information contained within this book, either directly or indirectly.

Legal Notice:

This book is copyright protected. It is only for personal use. You cannot amend, distribute, sell, use, quote or paraphrase any part, or the content within this book, without the consent of the author or publisher.

Disclaimer Notice:

Please note the information contained within this document is for educational and entertainment purposes only. All effort has been executed to present accurate, up to date, reliable, complete information. No warranties of any kind are declared or implied. Readers acknowledge that the author is not engaged in the rendering of legal, financial, medical or professional advice. The content within this book has been derived from various sources. Please consult a licensed professional before attempting any techniques outlined in this book.

By reading this document, the reader agrees that under no circumstances is the author responsible for any losses, direct or indirect, that are incurred as a result of the use of the information contained within this document, including, but not limited to, errors, omissions, or inaccuracies.

Table of Contents

INTRODUCTION 1

CHAPTER 1: IT'S NOT JUST IN YOUR HEAD 7

    THINK AGAIN 7
    THE DOMINO EFFECT STARTS 10
    POTENTIAL HEALTH CONSEQUENCES 15
    THE EXTERNAL ENVIRONMENT 21

CHAPTER 2: HOW DID YOU GET HERE? 27

    THE BASIS OF ORIGIN 27
    CHILDHOOD ROOTS 31
    ENVIRONMENTAL CONDITIONING 35
    AN ADDICTIVE ILLUSION 39

CHAPTER 3: THE DEMONS IN YOUR MIND 45

    THE TRUE FACE OF NEGATIVE THINKING 45
    DISTORTED PROSPECTS 50
    RECOGNIZING ANTS 59

CHAPTER 4: FIGHTING OFF THE DEMONS 63

    A FUNDAMENTAL CHANGE 63
    STOP NEGATIVE SELF-TALK 68
    SWIFT BATTLE PLANS 71
    TRAINING PLANS 75

CHAPTER 5: PROTECTING YOUR MIND 81

    SECRETS TO A BEAUTIFUL MIND 81
    THREE FOUNDATIONAL PRACTICES 87
    THE FOURTH FUNDAMENTAL 93

CHAPTER 6: ACCEPTING AND LOVING YOURSELF 101

A Resistant Relationship 101
  Much Needed Care 106
  Nutrition for the Self 109

CHAPTER 7: YOU'RE IN CONTROL 115

  Mind Your Control 115
  Mastering Your Mind 117
  Step-by-Step Control 121
  The Toolkit 126

CONCLUSION 129

REFERENCES 133

Introduction

Willie Nelson once said, "Once you replace negative thoughts with positive ones, you'll start having positive results." This sounds simple, doesn't it? However, you wouldn't be here if it was that simple. Negative thinking is like a vacuum that traps you. It doesn't change just by thinking yourself out of the vacuum. It requires long-term changes, because let's face it, your patterns of thought haven't manifested overnight. Negativity weighs heavy on your mind. You feel like you're dragging a bus behind you, and this incredible weight doesn't make the road forward any easier. Every time the road evens out a bit, another negative thought pops into your mind to make your load even heavier to pull. It's no wonder you feel held back in life. It's just one consequence of pessimism.

Before you know it, you feel unworthy, unappreciated, unloved, unproductive, and unattractive. Your confidence feels like it fell off the bus at the last turn. Your self-esteem is as low as a loosely vapored cloud hanging over your head. You start doubting everything you can do, think, and feel. You're not sure if you can ever be successful, happy, or healthy. Judgment slides into the driver seat of the bus you're pulling, and suddenly, you start degrading yourself for your mistakes and perceived failures. The voice of self-judgment kicks you when you're down. Now, you're echoing the same doubts you subtly heard deep in your mind. You become withdrawn and isolated because you can't meet the standards of what passes for attractive now. You can't even make small talk, so your date will laugh. You rather choose not to meet them, and loneliness sneaks into your life.

You start questioning your ability to become an entrepreneur. You can't even do things right at work, so how are you supposed to be successful on your own? The voices grow louder, and the thoughts come at you with unfathomable speeds. You stop enjoying the activities you loved before because your thoughts won't allow you to feel good anymore. Your emotions are all over the place, and you aren't functioning at your best. You think you can always be better. In one sense, you can, but in another sense, your ability to ruminate on what you don't like about yourself is preventing you from taking action. Your mind is so far from the truth, which is that you're amazing as you are right now. Your mind won't let you focus on the qualities you possess. It won't allow you access to happy memories and accomplishments.

It keeps pulling you back because you eventually think you can't untether yourself from the 16-ton bus behind you. Your self-belief and confidence wither as your mind continues to trap you with this unbearable weight. Before long, your mental health takes a dip, and your physical health soon follows. You can't understand why you're getting sick all the time, and you can't explain the depression that seeped in out of nowhere. That's where you're mistaken. Depression and anxiety can follow negativity, and mental health disorders only bring more negativity. The interconnected relationship between depression and negativity was confirmed again in a study of 160 people published in the *International Journal of Psychology* (Mohammadkhani et al., 2018).

The relationship between depression and overall health must be considered if you're experiencing physical symptoms. The mind and body are intertwined in a delicate relationship, so what happens in the mind can affect the body and vice versa. The human mind is the control center of everything that goes right and wrong in your body. It controls the way you feel and how you respond to negative and positive situations. You're also not the only person struggling with this relationship. Your state of mind is influenced by an accumulation of things, just like everyone else's. The news is just one influencer, even though we're impacted by all the happenings in our communities, experiences, workplaces, and social crowds. However, news has been the frontrunning negative influencer during the pandemic.

According to statistics released in early 2021, negative influences are swarming our minds (Djordjevic, 2021). The news consists of 95% sensationalism today, and 87% of the coronavirus news coverage was negative in 2020. Negative news is also 30% more likely to catch your attention, and 26.7% of people develop anxiety from news stories. These figures are outrageous because 10% of Americans watch the news every hour, whether it's on social media or television. The figures don't improve, especially when you learn that a Russian news website lost 66% of its viewers after publishing positive stories for one day. The silver lining here is that you've noticed you don't want to be negative anymore. You're realized how it holds you back in life and how the cycle becomes inescapable if you're stuck in it for too long.

Maybe you didn't know where to find help, or you never had anyone to turn to, but you recognize how your self-doubt is sabotaging your ability to function normally. You want to stop overthinking and enjoy life again. You want to change, have better self-esteem, and exude confidence. You want to start believing people who compliment you and your work. You may have a burning desire to get out of your head and achieve the best quality of life. If you want to think and feel better in this crazy world, it's time to learn about negativity and what it does to you. Negativity has scientific and psychological effects on your body, emotions, mental clarity, and even your motivation. Everything is influenced by the powerful human mind, but knowing what can happen also helps you avoid it.

You'll also learn the reasons you keep having negative thoughts, even when you desire something better. This helps you embrace the upcoming changes with the right approach because you can't just start thinking positively. You'll learn why this doesn't work. Negative thoughts have a purpose in some sense, and you'll find out what that purpose is. Your mind is an incredibly intricate machine, and nothing happens without a purpose. You'll also understand how to identify and differentiate your negative thinking patterns because not all of them are equal. Some negative thoughts might even be beneficial under controlled circumstances. Once you spot the enemy, you can charge against it, and you'll be better prepared to win the battle.

Getting out of a negative cycle can seem daunting, impossible, and downright vicious, but you can do much more than you think. Your beliefs are a little wounded right now, but you can stand up and fight again. You won't just learn how to win the battle, but you'll also have a good standing in the war as you learn to protect your mind against the fallout that comes with negative thinking patterns. Your mind will be prepared for the long haul, and this will only make you stronger. Your mind can be the instigator for a life worth living if you just give it a chance. Giving up is not an option, irrespective of what comes your way. Teaching the mind to protect itself will prevent you from falling back into old habits.

You'll find a myriad of mental self-care tools that will allow you to reconnect with the authentic side of your mind. You'll familiarize yourself with the different characters who encourage your behaviors, and strengthening these relationships opens new doors. You'll learn to love yourself and your mind for the powerful qualities it possesses, and you'll find the secret to controlling your mind consciously. The subconscious mind has driven your behaviors and responses long enough. You can practice a new way of life, and it only requires a little dedication. Discipline your mind, and you'll become the master of your thoughts. And when everything seems too overwhelming, you'll know when to seek professional help. There's nothing wrong with finding the right assistance when the world seems too demanding.

I've been in your shoes and faced many of the same demons. Negativity nearly ruined my quality of life. Its purpose was to diminish the life of which I could be proud one day when I'm a gray man sitting on my porch. I faced many challenges in my life that would've set many people back, but I pushed forth until I started studying the human mind. I was fascinated by the clockwork brain, and how it functions. I learned how the human mind is the center of my universe, and after five years of rigorous research from scientific resources, I knew I could change the way I thought. I knew I could master the mind and remove the limitations set by an uncontrolled mind. I understand your pain, and I know how mental health issues can feel unbearable, but I promise you this: you can master your mind.

I've written numerous books in this same series, and they comb over the finer details connecting mental health and the human mind. It's been my passion over these five years, and I wish to help you find a solution to your problems now, too. You're far stronger than you believe, but your beliefs might try to convince you otherwise. If you feel the burning urge to become your mental master, dive into the first chapter to unravel the mind's mysteries.

Chapter 1:

It's Not Just in Your Head

The magnitude of our thoughts defines the significance of our overall well-being and success. Your thoughts have a greater impact on your life than you think. They are the fuel that fills your brain, mind, and body with the energy to choose directions in your life, including your health. Thoughts can change your emotional, mental, and physical health in ways you're most likely unaware. The subtlety of what goes on in the mind, often below our conscious awareness, can unfold our future in positive or negative ways. Thoughts are constantly chattering away, and you won't have a grasp on your future health or success unless you intentionally become aware of them.

Think Again

If for some reason, even after purchasing this book that indicates the first stage of awareness, you still don't believe you're negative enough to alter your outcomes, then you should think again. Only once you see the subtle but persistent thoughts that often go unnoticed, can you identify the frequency you may be using negative thoughts to navigate your days. You may be familiar with many of these thoughts. Again, you wouldn't be reading this if you weren't becoming aware of them. However, some thoughts may surprise you. Consider for a moment how often you think in these ways.

"I'm not good enough." This thought is a sign of low self-esteem, which defines the way we respect, value, and feel confident about ourselves.

"I can't do this." The word *can't* should be stricken from the English language. What you speak is what you believe, so you're limiting yourself every time you use this word.

"I don't think I can ever do that." The word *think* is the problem here. You shouldn't be basing your decisions on whether you think you can do something. If you know something, then it's a valid thought. If you tried it before, and your method failed, you know you're not able to do this. However, that also doesn't mean you can't try a different method. Thinking about your abilities is a clear sign that you have no experience in trying the task you fear.

"No one cares about me." This is a "drawing-straws" statement. Everyone shows their emotions differently, and assuming no one cares about you is bound to make you feel unworthy.

"I'm not intelligent enough." This is a common negative thought, and it merely shows that you're comparing yourself to someone. Who do you want to be smarter than? Are you capable of completing your tasks at work and home? Comparing yourself to others in any form is a negative thought, which you'll learn more about soon enough.

"I'm a failure if I don't succeed perfectly." Perfection is a massive fallacy, and failure only happens when a lack of trying precedes it.

"Bad things always happen to me." This thought is like lying on train tracks and accepting your fate to be crushed by a train. Self-acceptance is a powerful part of being an optimist, but accepting bad things without realizing you have some control can be detrimental. You can control your thoughts, meaning you won't lie down on the track.

"I should be eating healthier." *Should* thoughts indicate that you're giving up before you start. The word has the same connotations as 'maybe.' It also displaces you in the future where you have no control. You're undermining your abilities when you say *should*. Instead, you should be saying "I can eat healthier."

Now, you've had a chance to think again. Do you think you're a little negative, or can you see yourself having these thoughts all day, every day? Negative thoughts affect your thinking patterns and the way you feel about yourself, life, health, and the future. However, it doesn't stop there. Negative thoughts have a domino effect throughout your life.

The Domino Effect Starts

Once you admit how negative you may be, you need to learn about what this state of mind can do to your health, mind, brain, body, success, career, and self-esteem among others. Negative thoughts cascade from your mental to your emotional and physical states. Being pessimistic can change the structure and functions of your brain, which affect the rest of your body and mind (Wolff, 2019). It all starts with a little chemical called cortisol, which is released from the hypothalamus-pituitary-adrenal (HPA) axis. The hypothalamus is ignited by the emotional amygdala region in your brain, which is housed within the limbic system inside the middle of the brain. The hypothalamus then sends signals to the pituitary glands, which then communicate with the adrenal glands, and you have a cascading biochemical effect in your brain and body when cortisol and adrenaline are coursing through your veins and neural pathways.

Your central nervous system (CNS) and bloodstream are impacted by what may seem like a small bump of cortisol every time you think negatively. What happens when you take small steps toward a finish line? They eventually accumulate to create progress. Now, the small bumps of cortisol aren't accumulating progress.

They're doing the opposite. Cortisol is a natural stress chemical, but an excess of it can cause a host of health issues. Its intention is to fight stress, but negative thoughts are mostly not considered stress, even though they make the brain fearful. Acting as a neurotransmitter in the brain, cortisol can wreak havoc on the structure of the largest organ in your body. The brain is a malleable organ that changes with experience. It's changing every moment of your life. The changes, called neuroplasticity and neurogenesis, are highly influenced by what flows through the synapses and neurons in the brain.

Neurons are the billions of cells within the brain, and synapses are the connections between them. Neuroplasticity refers to the brain's ability to recognize preferred or repeated behaviors (chemical or thought), and the brain will adapt to strengthen and weaken certain connections between two neurons. Neurogenesis refers to the death and regeneration of neurons or cells, which is a natural process. One structural change that happens in the brain is when white matter increases versus gray matter. White matter is named as such for its white coloration on brain scans. It shows an area of the brain that's denser with synapses surrounded by myelin. Gray matter shows darker on scans, and it indicates areas of the brain where more neurons are present. White matter can also indicate habitual connections between specific brain regions, whereas gray matter shows a lack of connections.

However, gray matter is the preferred highlight in the brain. White matter indicates that certain brain regions are overworked and others aren't being used as they must be. Gray matter shows a better allocation of resources from all the brain regions. Neuronal activity is far less efficient in white matter versus active gray matter. Negative thoughts can also increase your white matter, and this means you won't have all your brain regions active and firing when you feel stressed. Your responses will decline due to the slow movements in white matter. The cerebellum, or small brain, slows down during negative thought patterns, too. This causes an issue when you're trying to process complex thoughts and solve problems. Beyond your brain working slower and you not being able to use the advantage of multiple regions required for higher thinking, negativity continues to knock down valuable structures in the brain.

The frontal lobe, or particularly the prefrontal cortex (PFC), also doesn't thrive under these conditions (Reynolds & Aubele, 2011). The prefrontal cortex is the higher-thinking seat above your brain, and it lies just behind the forehead. This is the region that chooses what you value based on what you pay attention to and how your emotions react. The more you pay attention to negativity, fears, and habitual cynicism, the greater the connections will grow between the PFC and the emotional regions of your brain, bypassing the logical side. The synapses and neurons between the regions will further multiply and coat themselves for lasting communication, and your negative thought processes will be reinforcing themselves with each new thought. The prefrontal cortex organizes decisions and controls cognitive functions, and it's losing energy, which is diverted elsewhere when you're negative.

You can't think clearly when your PFC isn't functioning as well as it should. This will affect your behavior and decisions, which impacts the amount of success you achieve in the world. The left side of the prefrontal cortex is mostly used by optimists because believe it or not, optimism is hard work for the brain. However, hard work pays off in everything we think and do. Optimism requires a compilation of creativity, higher thinking, motivation, and emotional components. Without the left side of your PFC working correctly, this processing is impacted as negatively as your mood. Lost attention and a slower brain lead to an inability to problem-solve. Think about how often this happens, considering how the brain is undeniably impacted by the stress hormones.

The hippocampus region of the brain is where the majority of your influential memories are stored. This is the region that stores habitual emotional tones and descriptions created in your mind and thoughts. Your higher thinking is also where your conscious mind and awareness are, and the descriptions chosen by the PFC are then stored deep within the hippocampus region, which then rewires your brain to create stronger synapses and neural pathways. What you commonly think and feel in any situation, stressful or not, is what designs the deeply embedded habits within the brain. They can become so ingrained into your neural network that it requires proper and timeous dismantling to undo the negative patterns. Rewiring your brain back to the positive side is possible with some effort though.

The hypothalamus residing in the thalamus region decides what's threatening or not, depending on what information it receives from the amygdala and habitual descriptions in the brain. The problem with the chemical instigator is that it can't differentiate between true threats and insignificant fears caused by negative thinking. It relies on using information from the other regions to respond to any given situation. Once the stress hormones flow into your central nervous system and body, physical changes take place, such as an increased blood pressure and heart rate. Once you physically feel unwell due to the stress response changing your vital signs, however subtle it may seem, you will become increasingly worried or anxious. In the least, your anxiety rises, and you'll find it difficult to process thoughts clearly.

Complex processing relies on all systems functioning well, so you may feel foggy when you have to make a decision. You may feel depressed because fears become more genuine as this cascading effect touches every part of your perception. You may feel hesitant or start thinking even worse of yourself. The bottom line is that what happens in the brain can impact the body, and what happens in the body can influence the brain. Your thoughts control your brain, which impacts your moods and physical sensations. Your physical symptoms can return the effect to the brain, creating a cycle. Your body, mind, and brain work together, and any change to one system will affect another one.

Potential Health Consequences

Many negative emotions like anger, fear, and frustration can become a serious cause for concern when you adopt them as a permanent disposition. They will change your outlook on the world to make you only see the thin lines between everything positive. This is a habit you don't want to possess. You don't want to focus on the person dying on the news and ignore the children's school bus that was rescued successfully from the lake. You don't want to constantly think how much the persistent rain is stopping you from visiting the beach and ignore the need for it after a long drought. You don't want to turn to imagined assumptions when your boss calls you to his office but ignore the email you received from a client to thank you for a great service.

Every situation has a positive and negative undertone if you look close enough, and focusing on the hints of potential negativity can keep you from being healthy and successful. Each time you ruminate about walking into your boss' office, you're pushing your blood pressure up, and you're preventing your creative and logical minds from taking center stage. Every time you think the doctor has bad news and you delay the call, you're putting your heart under greater strain. Who knows? The doctor might have good news. Pause your expectations for a moment, and recognize how you may be harming yourself more than anything else. Our thoughts and emotions have a widespread impact on every part of our health, including the metabolism, immune system, and bodily hormones.

Negative thoughts and emotions come naturally, following a tragedy, heartbreak, or trauma, but they shouldn't be consistent in your daily life. You may start experiencing some of the physical symptoms common after a negatively induced stress response, such as headaches, fatigue, digestive issues, and chest pain. Our brains are designed to protect us against threats, dangers, and any situation that could upset the balance of our lives, so it's understandable that the stress response activates when you ruminate on negative thoughts. The way our brains work is negatively biased because the world was once full of threats and dangers. We aren't born negative, but it's simpler to focus on the negative side because we want to protect ourselves. Negativity bias is great when we look both ways before crossing a street, but it becomes counterproductive when we rely on it after minor disputes with loved ones, being called into our employer's office, or sitting in traffic.

Over time, the health effects from an overactive negativity bias can lead to chronic stress, which has numerous potentially dangerous consequences, according to Doctor Karen Lawson (2012). Chronic stress can prevent the body and brain from harmonizing the hormones required to maintain homeostasis, which is when your internal environment remains consistent. Any disruptions in the environment within your body and brain can trigger an avalanche of physical and emotional symptoms. You start lacking resilience, which makes you unable to bounce back to your normal internal environment after a setback. Once resilience is flawed, chronic stress continues to blossom, changing the way your health unfolds. Your brain will be depleted of the chemicals it needs to restore itself and strengthen the pathways between regions you require and desire.

The stress hormones can also impact your immune system if they aren't managed in chronic stress. The immune system is responsible for inflammation and reparation throughout your brain and body, and chronic stress can progress this process, leaving inflammation to grow wildly throughout your system. Mismanaged inflammation has a counter-effect on the immune system. Think about a truck. What happens when you stop adding gas to the tank but you keep driving it? Eventually, you'll run out of gas because it can't run off fumes. You'll be stuck on the side of the road, but all you had to do was fill the gas tank. Gas is very much like rest, which are the gaps between stress responses. You can't fill your brain with gas, but you can rest it from the physiological response that follows stress.

Doctor Lawson also shares what might be the most significant finding in science to date. Chronic stress harms the telomere strands at the end of our genes. The length of these strands is used to predict longevity, and stress can shorten them. Being negative may shorten your lifespan, especially if you're constantly under pressure. Keep in mind that stress isn't always easy to recognize. You may just feel tired today, and it could be an underlying symptom of stress. Unhelpful thoughts may be active in your subconscious mind, which is below your awareness, but it doesn't change the fact that you're responding to them. That's why it's so important to recognize our thoughts. Thinking is a natural process, and we can't always evaluate our thoughts unless we choose to focus on them.

Ask yourself, do you want to live long and prosper? If you do, negative thinking won't bring you any closer to a long life. Your mental health can be restructured with negative thinking. Chronic stress, anxiety, and depression become higher risks for you. Depression can also lead to type two diabetes, heart problems, and disability. If you're wondering why depression can lead back to physical ailments, you simply have to remember that your emotions affect every other part of your body, including your stress response. The cycle is a nightmare, and the lower your happy hormones decline, the higher your probability of depression becomes. If you can't follow the light in your life, however faint it may be, you're at risk for serious health problems.

Heart disease is something we all know about and want to avoid, but negativity can change your relationship with your heart. A study of over 97,000 women was published in *Circulation*, which shines truth on the relationship between negative thoughts and heart disease (Tindle et al., 2009). The women were divided into two main groups. One group of women were optimistic, and the other group were either cynic or hostile. Cynicism is when you're skeptical about the possibility of good outcomes. Hostile means you're unfriendly toward others. Cynicism and hostility are common traits among pessimists. All the women were healthy at the time the study began. None of them had cardiovascular problems. The Cook Medley Questionnaire and Life Orientation tests were used to divide the women.

The most cynical women in the above-mentioned study were struggling significantly more with coronary artery disease (CAD) after eight years, and some of them even passed away before the study was completed. This study proves that pessimism not only increases your risk for heart disease, but it also gives more evidence again that it can shorten your lifespan. Both Caucasian and African-American women were examined, and the results were similar between pessimistic and optimistic women from both ethnic groups. The heart is a delicate organ, and constant stress caused by negative thought patterns can impact the heart's ability to function as it should. You're putting strain on your heart every time your heart rate increases. You're making it work overtime when your blood pressure rises. Logically, the heart can't withstand all the pressure.

Another study published in *Stroke: A Journal of Cerebral Circulation* examined how negative thinking contributes to an increased risk for stroke (Emerson-Rose et al., 2014). The focus was on a condition called atherosclerosis, which is the increasing build-up of plaque in the arteries, and it's related to the heart as well. As the plaque increases, the arteries become narrowed and overburdened. Clots can form, and the plaque may rupture as the clot tries to move through the artery. This could happen anywhere in your body, including the brain, which leads to a stroke. The ruptured artery leading into the brain can deprive it of receiving oxygen, which it needs to function and survive. Anyway, the study focused on how pessimism was one of the contributing factors to heighten the risk of atherosclerosis, and it was proven to be a viable cause of stroke.

Degenerative disorders are also on the rise thanks to negative thinking patterns. A recent study published in *Alzheimer's and Dementia* showed how pessimism can age and decline the brain (Marchant et al., 2020). Anxiety and depression already increase your risk for dementia, which is the cognitive decline of neurons and gray matter in the brain. It's a degenerative disease without a cure. You start losing brain functions, such as memory and judgment, because the regions slowly start diminishing. The study was conducted at University College London, and they took a different approach to examine the connection between dementia and pessimism.

Negative thinking patterns often precede anxiety and depression, and the researchers focused on two key proteins used to determine whether someone will develop dementia. Three hundred people participated in the study over two years, of which 113 participants had amyloid-positron emission tomography (PET) scans done to see whether they had the protein markers. They were asked how they feel about certain scenarios that would either encourage negative or positive responses. The participants who expressed negative worries and emotions were showing significantly higher levels of tau and amyloid proteins in the brain. Their memory and cognitive decline were far more advanced than the optimistic participants. Ultimately, your risk for dementia and Alzheimer's increases when you spend your life in a pessimistic bubble.

All the potential health consequences of negativity can be avoided if you learn to slowly change your attitude. The brain doesn't actually see what information you consume. It relies on the descriptions you allocate to the information. Maintaining your brain's health will ensure improved physical and emotional health. Even emotional health must be tamed for better physical health, and the latter can also impact mental and emotional health. This is what could happen to your internal environment if you choose negativity, but it can extend further than this.

The External Environment

What happens to your life, work, and relationships that make up your external environment when you're always pessimistic? All the factors can be affected by your attitude toward them. According to a huge study of more than 30,000 participants in the United Kingdom, which was published in PLoS ONE, perception changes everything (Kindermann et al., 2013). Genetics, social, and experiential factors can change the way you cope with life and your mental health; pessimism can do the same. The results were astounding because they proved that events alone don't change the way you feel. It's your perception of what happened that makes the difference. The responses you have toward stressful situations can alter your mental well-being, which changes the risks of physical and emotional health.

Your perceptions, beliefs, and identity become what is known as your inner critic. There are two ways in which your external environment is affected by negativity, namely lifestyle habits and personal growth. The inner critic changes the way you make decisions, so it can impact your external environment as well. The inner critic is famously negative, and it's the voice you hear when you blame yourself, feel obsolete, question your decisions, and choose the wrong coping mechanisms for stressful situations. Suddenly, your lifestyle habits start changing because your inner critic frightens, limits, and shames you for reasons soon to be known. Doubt becomes an integral part of your new perspective. The inner critic starts telling you that you can't get promoted at work, you won't find love, and you aren't smart enough to solve a problem.

Moreover, this inner critic loves speaking up at night. Insomnia commonly exists among negative people because they can't silence their inner chatter. It's one of the most prevalent lifestyle habits that change, and sleeplessness only aggravates the problem. Insomnia leads to depression, anxiety, mood disorders, and physical illnesses because sleep is the time we need to restore ourselves. We store memories during sleep, and our bodies go through a restorative stage. Other lifestyle habits that may change with negativity driving your inner voice are metabolic. You might turn to the wrong foods to cope with undesirable feelings and thoughts. You might start drinking and using narcotics to silence the endless chatter, but it never stops unless you change the attitude of the voice. Smoking is another common coping mechanism when we perceive life as a bowl of worms, and it comes with its own consequences.

Your personal growth will remain stagnant, or worse, it will deteriorate because you're overwhelmed by limited thoughts, self-doubts, and self-destructive behaviors. Your ability to capitalize on opportunities will diminish once you're too afraid of the untruths spoken by the inner critic. You'll be living in a bubble that prevents you from taking chances to grow and improve, and your declining brain regions will only make it harder to use your logical mind. Emotions will roam free with your thoughts, and you'll be stuck before you know it. Your career and relationships won't thrive in these conditions. You'll become socially withdrawn, which only amplifies your negative thoughts and feelings. The negativity trap and the inner critic's constant chatter can see you entering a spiral from which it's hard to surface if you don't realize what they're doing to you.

Think about it like this. You walk into a restaurant, and you notice someone staring at you. The first thought that pops into your mind is that this person must find you amusingly unattractive. A few seconds later, the person continues staring at you, and you feel the pressure bubbling up. No, they must think you're hideous. Suddenly, they burst into laughter while their eyes are still latched onto you. Now, all the worst thoughts are running through your mind. You must be fat, monstrous, and disgusting. That's the only reason they're laughing. All this time, your logical mind is struggling to make its way to the opportunity of this situation. This woman is sitting with who may be her best friend. Her friend just told her a joke, but you're so defensive thanks to your negative inner voice that you didn't think she may be looking at you out of interest.

Negativity is a perpetual monster. It can take a harmless situation and turn it into something unreal. Negativity can also be perpetually harmful in the opposite direction if you're thinking the woman is jealous of you, or perhaps you think people should pay more attention to you. You might feel unappreciated or invisible, two feelings that could quickly harm any relationship, especially if they're ill-perceived. Negativity can turn beautiful opportunities into something your dog wouldn't eat. Don't allow pessimism to ruin your internal or external environment. Negative thinking is a massive determining factor for where you'll end up in this life, and you don't have to be a hostage to your thoughts.

The thoughts themselves aren't your ideas or values, but they're ideas and values we've learned to accept from the past. These ideas and values shape our identities and give credence to the inner critic. Know your enemy, and you'll know how to dethrone the inner critic.

Chapter 2:

How Did You Get Here?

A maple tree planted in the swamp or thin, rocky soil cannot thrive, but plant the same tree in clay-like or loose soil, and you have a beautiful giant in the making. No one starts life with a negative perspective. It's usually developed through our experiences, some of which we have control and many of which we don't. Our experiences are the soil that nurtures our growth, well-being, and success. Much of our experiences are instilled by others, and some experiences are chosen, especially once we grow accustomed to the soil provided by other people. Negativity has complicated roots itself, and understanding how you got here can help you nurture your mind with new experiences and better thoughts.

The Basis of Origin

There isn't a person in this world who doesn't have negative thoughts running through their minds, but the way we think about it and the way we perceive an experience determines how happy, secure, successful, and healthy we remain. Negative thoughts can be the sinkhole that engulfs your tree, or you can learn to manage them better so you continue to nurture the soil you'll be rooted in for the rest of your days. Change is always possible, no matter where you stand right now, but it begins with knowing what negative thoughts truly look like. It's time to unmask the basis of origins for negative thinking patterns. Negative thoughts are often one of three kinds.

First, you may be worried about the present and all that's happening right now. Everything happening around you at any moment is a possible cause for negative thoughts. There might be negative events unfolding, such as natural disasters, broken relationships, or personal perceived failure. Stock market crashes, unemployment numbers rising, and the current news can influence your anxiety about the present. It's all an experience you're living through in real-time.

Second, your negative thoughts might be coming from past experiences, such as trauma, abuse, or regret. Most of us have experienced and done things we're not proud of mentioning. We may even feel ashamed and embarrassed about our past. Perhaps you were in an abusive relationship, and now the memory defines your self-worth. Maybe you hurt someone's feelings, and you blame yourself for being insensitive. The past can also alter your thought patterns.

Third, the future is but another fear we can conjure, and it commonly concerns most people. You may start questioning your abilities and see yourself as a guaranteed failure when the future unfolds in your mind. You think you can't be a great success, you will only be a failure in your marriage, or you'll likely lose your home investment because this city was hit by a hurricane 20 years ago. This is where it gets complicated because future fears and negative thoughts can be influenced by past experiences. It's even possible to fear all three timelines at once.

Everyone experiences the fears of past, present, and future, but when they become consistent enough to alter your thinking patterns, then you have a problem. If your primary focus is on the fears and uncertainties within these timelines, you have some work to do. Have you ever wondered why negativity bias is hardwired into the brain? The simple answer is that it was necessary for the days where cavemen dwelled on the earth. Back then, it was a case of eat or be eaten. You either had to fight or flee from danger. There weren't reinforced doors protecting cavemen from the dangers outside their caves. A dangerous animal could enter the cave in the middle of the night and eat them.

At this point in human history, it was a matter of life and death to focus on the dangers, threats, bad stuff, and negative possibilities. The cavemen who paid better attention and were attuned to danger were the ones who survived. Unfortunately, as genetic evolution works, the survivors are our ancient forefathers, and they're the same primitive people who passed the genes down to our cultures, even though we don't need to watch our backs in case a wild animal jumps out of nowhere. Well, criminals may resemble wild animals, but society has become quite civilized and doesn't need extreme threat detection anymore. Irrespective, the genes that make us more attentive to danger are within our physiology, and that's how our negativity bias was created. It's in our nature to focus on the negative before the positive.

This psychological evolution explains why we tend to have lingering effects after a negative event. Take first impressions as an example. It's nearly impossible for you to like someone who left a bad taste in your mouth when you first met. Therapy was designed to help people overcome trauma because the lingering effects of what happened can embed themselves into your mind, making you anxious or depressed. As humans, we tend to remember the traumatic experience more than positive events. We latch onto criticism before we accept praise, and we can more easily overreact to negative stimuli, news, and changes in our lives. We can vividly remember negative details, but positive details are simply forgotten. The average person has more negative thoughts daily than positive ones, even when they aren't aware of them.

One way negativity bias creeps upon us is when we respond more strongly to a negative event than we would to an equally positive event. Let's say you're on a date with someone new. She is pretty and well-spoken, and she makes you laugh. The two of you seem to have similar interests, and you can imagine yourself on a second date. Suddenly, she says something that turns the tables. You find out that she doesn't eat seafood, which you love. Now, that's all you can think about. You start knit-picking for information about why she hates seafood, and all she says is that it tastes disgusting. Your belief that seafood is the greatest source of nutrition in the world is so overpowering that you forget how she makes you laugh. You forget about her gorgeous smile. All you can focus on is that you won't be able to dine at a seafood restaurant, and the second date never happens.

The negativity bias was intended to protect us from danger at the start of evolution, but now we use it to decide whether we'll speak to someone again. The attractive women may have been the best relationship you would've entered, but you allowed your bias to forget the positive things. You must realize that humans no longer face life and death situations daily, and they don't need to dwell on the negative side anymore. Everyone has this bias ingrained into their minds, so what allows some people to see the positive aspects of an experience while others are blinded by the negative side? This is where experience comes into play. Your experiences have either amplified or nullified your negativity bias.

Childhood Roots

The first experiences you thrive upon or survive are in childhood, and these can set the pace for negative thinking if you were merely a survivor. Every experience we have is wiring our brains from the moment we first enter this world. A neglected baby who cries endlessly without receiving nurture and love from their parents is bound to have a subliminal thought pop into their mind as adults. They'll wonder if they're worth anything because their parents didn't think so. An abused child will always wonder whether they can amount to anything because everything they do is wrong. The words our parents speak to us when we make mistakes and a lack of encouragement after a stumble can set the stage for low self-esteem and self-doubt. Suddenly, we fear all timelines in our adult lives because we weren't capable of achieving greatness and perfection as children.

We might have been compared to other children; sometimes, it could have been our siblings. Maybe we were compared to friends or classmates by our teachers, who also established influential experiences in childhood. Our parents may be our first teachers, but our school teachers have a huge impact on our lives, especially when they say stupid things to children who absorb everything.

Why can't you listen for once?

What's wrong with you?

I told you to do it this way!

I must share a story of a young boy who fits well into this paradigm. He was a creative little guy, and his excitement was abundant in preschool. One day in class, his teacher asked them to paint a picture. The little boy was ecstatic and started painting a red car. Suddenly, the teacher yelled at him for starting before she could tell him what to paint. She wanted a flower with a green stem and yellow petals.

The boy conformed to his teacher's wishes. Two weeks later, the teacher excited the boy again by telling the class it was time to create something with clay. The boy began creating a dog, but the teacher again yelled at him for his ignorance and haste. She wanted a vase, and so he created one. This went on for months before the boy moved to another town. At his new school, the teacher asked the class to paint a picture. After a few minutes passed, the teacher walked over to the boy to ask him why he wasn't painting. The boy then told her that he didn't know what to paint. She said he could paint anything, but the boy felt nervous. He wanted her to tell him what to paint. The moral of this story is that every experience in childhood is molding us into a new perspective. This boy's creative perspective was crushed by a negative teacher, and so, he adopted her attitude toward art.

Anyway, teachers, parents, friends, and relatives are constantly shaping our perceptions and beliefs in this world while we're too young to have our own. Childhood is 18 years of experiences that make us think in certain ways. Our negativity bias is being shaped by the first bully we encounter and the first relative who compares us to our siblings or cousins because they don't believe in us. Your seeds are being planted in soil that isn't conducive to your growth and development.

You become negative because of your experiences. Your experiences that enhance negative thinking aren't always as blatant as a mother asking you to be more like a sibling who perceivably behaves better. It's not always as blatant as a bully pushing you around the playground.

Your negativity bias might not be as powerful as it is based solely on an abusive childhood where your father spanked you for not listening as well as he expects from you. Physical, emotional, and mental abuse can lead to children suffering from chronic stress and nervousness. An abusive environment during childhood is one of the most prominent and evident reasons we become negative, but there are subliminal inceptions among the evident reasons. These are the reasons we must think hard about. They're not as easy to recognize because they take the form of parents being too busy to help you through troubles. Parents overlooking your emotional needs can also instill negativity. Even your friends during childhood and in your adult life could be using subliminal inception to instill negativity.

A friend may envy you deep down, and they could sabotage your performance in school because they don't want to be outshined. Your parents may have been negative about their lives, and you learned from them as role models. Your father always doubted his chances of starting his own business, so he never did. Your mother believed she was incapable of being a good mother, so she never was. Your sister had no confidence to pursue her dreams, so she never went to college. Colleagues can also make you doubt yourself and your work in adulthood by dropping hints that start with the word 'but.' Doubts, guilt, shame, and negativity are the soil you're planted in as a child, and it continues throughout adulthood.

Our experiences with the people around us can change the way we think. It can make us overlook positive aspects of events and experiences to see what may be minor negativities. Your childhood is one of the main reasons you think the way you do.

Environmental Conditioning

The environment we live in can change the way we think as well. It changes our mental health, which can further exacerbate the tendency to think negatively. It's long been known that the environment influences the way we feel, and our emotions can make us change our perceptions of the world (Alliant International University, 2019). The biopsychosocial model of psychology factors in our environment, experiences, biology, and social well-being to clarify what changes our mindsets. Quite simply, we start thinking negatively because we're surrounded by it. From the news to the changes in government, everything is slowly shifting our minds into deeper negative waters if we don't become aware of it and choose to change it. Environmental factors that could promote more negativity include physical and social aspects.

The physical environment refers to anything that could change the biochemistry inside your brain and body, either directly or indirectly. Toxins, pollution, extreme weather, and smoking are direct causes of changes in your body and brain. Sleep deprivation is an indirect environmental cause because it's internal. Physical environmental influence can come in the form of a toxic or hazardous work environment that creates additional stress. It can be the foods you eat and lifestyle habits you practice. It can be anything in your physical environment that increases your stress levels to cause changes in your brain. Poverty is just another notch on the negativity belt because it causes negative emotions that lead to fear and doubt. It places strain on the present and future. Uncertainties can play a huge role in how negative you feel.

The socio-environmental influence that changes our perceptions and tendency to be negative comes in the form of relationships, community, careers, and purpose. Being surrounded by toxic people in adulthood is just as harmful as the childhood factor. Stepping into the arena of adulthood doesn't change the influence your social environment has over you. The jealous friends may still be around, or you may have new ones. Toxic friends are commonly attracted to people with low self-esteem. It allows them to feed off your joy and steal your positivity while they plant more negative seeds in your mind. They'll make you feel worse about yourself, and they'll try to put you down with every chance they get. Toxic friends only focus on elevating themselves.

They don't care about your growth, and they turn you into a negative person.

Sometimes, workplaces aren't toxic or hazardous in a physical sense. You might be surrounded by colleagues who take advantage of you. Your boss might always overlook you when promotions are available because they don't appreciate you. A lack of appreciation, which goes both ways, is a sure sign of a toxic relationship. One way toxic employers love putting their employees down is by making them feel inferior. Your risks of becoming negative grow with every toxic relationship in your life. A lack of meaningful work, relationships, supportive friends, and even hobbies can make life seem like an uphill battle. And what does stress do? It pushes you into the negative corner. Other social environmental factors that could be elevating your negativity include the lack of spiritual or religious affiliation.

Spiritualism makes you feel like you're a part of something better, bigger, and meaningful. It helps you realize that you have a purpose, and being part of something better leads to hope. Hope is a powerful tool against negativity. Surrounding yourself with a social support group that shares your interests, values, and positive intentions can also challenge the negativity bias. Lacking social support from genuine people who challenge and reciprocate your good intentions can make the world seem overbearing. We all need someone to cheer us on, and we need people to believe in us. We aren't seeking validation, but it's wonderful to have someone recognize and appreciate us. Without having friends and relatives we can trust and appreciate ourselves, negativity is bound to simmer and keep us anxious.

The final piece of the environmental puzzle is self-care and relaxation. It's challenging to remain positive when we lack what our minds and bodies need. We need emotional, physical, and mental self-care to allow positivity to enter our minds. Not looking after yourself is like quitting before you begin. It shows a lack of interest in yourself, and it will only make you feel worse. Consciously choosing not to wear the best outfit you possess to your interview is a sign that you lack confidence and self-worth. You're already setting a negative first impression, and if you recall, those tend to last. It affects your personal life, too. Standing in front of the mirror with your hair standing in all directions doesn't make you feel confident or positive.

However, self-care isn't just about being on top of your appearance; it's also about controlling your mental and emotional clarity. That's where relaxation and time for yourself matters. An overworked brain cannot be positive. It will always lean toward the emotional and negative side of any situation because it doesn't have the energy or motivation to use logic. Everything you do, experience, feel, and see around you during childhood and until this day is gradually wiring your brain to be negative or positive. The fact that it's an ongoing and never-ending process means you can do something to change your trajectory.

An Addictive Illusion

Would you believe that you're capable of becoming addicted to negative thinking and even suffering? It may sound like madness, but you're probably familiar with the tendency to replay negative and painful thoughts in your mind. The truth is that 80% of our thoughts are negative, and 95% of them are repetitive (Colier, 2019). How is it possible that our minds prefer the painful or negative thoughts above success and laughter? Uncontrolled negative thoughts aren't only habits; they're also an addiction because our brains believe something harmful is an advantage. Keep in mind that your brain's primary focus is to protect your homeostasis. It intends to keep you safe from any harm, and this could make your brain ruminate on events and even pains that allude you to thinking you can change them next time. Think of your brain's addiction to negativity as a false belief that every outcome can be controlled.

We love returning to our suffering or negative experiences, and yes, love is the right word. We're fundamentally trying to change the outcome of an experience by overthinking, ruminating, and dissecting the event that caused the way you think and feel. It's a fact that we can learn from our experiences if we think about them logically, but rumination is an entirely different level of thought. We believe we can understand the way we feel after an experience if we just think long and hard enough about it. We spend copious amounts of time overthinking what happened because we're sure we have control over the future. We strongly believe we can control things that may not be within our control. The truth is that we can only control our reactions and responses to an experience. We can't hop back and forth through timelines to change the outcomes of an experience.

Nonetheless, we still think we can alter or fix the outcome. That way, the negative thought will disappear, but that's the illusion. What is your first reaction when you pass a car crash on the interstate? You want to stop and investigate. You want to know what caused the accident, and by no means can you take your eyes off the scene, no matter how traumatizing it might be. Studying the scene and analyzing what happened may just help you prevent an accident yourself. That's the illusion of logic behind the reaction. However, what happens when you still experience an accident after believing you're invincible? Your illusion is shattered, and you become even more negative and analytical. The problem with focusing intently on our suffering is that we get caught in the illusion that we can change the outcome.

The only thing you're able to change is your response to any experience in the present moment. Paradoxically, holding onto negative experiences also allows us to keep in touch with our identities. We think our identities are designed by the experiences we had in life, and in some way, this is true. Experience certainly directs our identities, but it doesn't define us. That's where the wires get crossed again. Allowing our identities to define us is like believing we couldn't accomplish what we did if we didn't suffer the way we did. Our suffering has influenced us, and it might have motivated us, but it doesn't mean we have to suffer to accomplish greatness. Our identities are partly made of the experiences we had, but we can't allow them to be the only source of identity in our lives. Some people are so afraid of moving away from their suffering because they may forget who they were, but that's a lie.

Returning to our suffering, pain, and negative experiences allows us to feel like we're still connected to our identities and that we continue to exist. We start experiencing ourselves as separate from the world when we face decisions and problems. Our thoughts hold onto experiences from the past and anxieties about the future, preventing us from focusing on what's happening right here and now. This can prevent us from making decisions and solving problems. Negative thinking falsely makes us believe we're safe if we continue to control the environment, social factors, and every experience to come by making us focus on the worst-case scenarios. The problem is that our identities, self-worth, and internal narrative are constantly designed by our experiences, so when something bad happens as it so often does in this world, we become unable to respond appropriately. This only disappoints us, and our minds latch onto more negativity and self-defeating behaviors.

The idea or thought that any of us can control the outcome of never-ending changes in an evolving world is the biggest illusion of them all. Our addiction to negativity is biologically driven by the desire for us to feel better, but we end up feeling even worse when more disappointment and negative experiences unfold. At some point, we start suffering more than we need to. We become more negative than what is good for us. Life and the chaotic world that followed the coronavirus pandemic are way too unpredictable to think we have control over outcomes. We can control our responses once we understand that it requires effort and time. Your mind will always choose to think about negative things rather than experience them, and this happens over and over. What happens when we experience the same thing repetitively? It becomes ingrained in our habits.

The problem with negative thoughts being perceived by the brain as beneficial to your well-being is that it responds with reinforcement. The brain releases reinforcing chemicals when you pay attention to negative thoughts (Pavlok, 2017). This explains why they become so addictive. Dopamine is a feel-good chemical that offers the same benefits as narcotics, and you're experiencing it each time you think negatively. Sure, stress hormones are also flowing about, but they're masked under dopamine. It's quite confusing for the brain, but this is how the brain reinforces the thoughts as habitual thinking patterns. You're being rewarded for repeating negative habits.

Your brain then stores and reinforces the connections within your basal ganglia, which is a collection of nuclei in the most primitive part of your brain. This is within the limbic system that also influences the way you think in the future. In other words, you're strengthening the connections that bypass the logical side of your prefrontal cortex. All habits are stored in this region, and incessant negative thinking will ensure that your emotional region is connected to your attention in the prefrontal cortex. The reason habits are so hard to change is that they're stored in this primitive region. Every time you have a negative thought, the connections between the habits are strengthened to produce the same effect next time. Think about any habit. Perhaps you have a habit of thinking people don't like you when you're in a social gathering.

This habitual thought keeps popping into your mind every time you're among people. Eventually, you don't even notice it anymore. It's just natural for you to feel awkward when people are around. You automatically believe people don't like you as you continue reinforcing the habit. The dopamine being released in the brain is what makes these habits stronger and stronger until they're officially addictions. One way to dissociate negative habits or thought patterns is to remove the pleasure factor. You can't just stop thinking no one likes you. You have to replace the thought with something else, or the brain will return to what allows the pleasure center to reinforce your habits again. However, we're getting ahead of ourselves now. Before you can tackle your negative thoughts, you need to understand what they are and how you can identify them.

Chapter 3:

The Demons in Your Mind

The voice of unreason may belong to an inner critic as sly as a demon. Inner voices aren't necessarily a sign of mental disorders. We all have the inner voice that makes us do things we may regret, and then we have the opposing voice that speaks rational thoughts into our minds. It's very much like the demon versus angel scenario on your shoulders. The demon is the inner critic. It's the voice that makes you doubt yourself and your abilities. It's the thoughts that hold you back from being your healthiest, happiest, and best self. This inner critic can be so loud that the rational angel has no way of communicating with you. You must know what the demon looks like so you can flick it off your shoulder to hear the rational voice speak louder.

The True Face of Negative Thinking

What is the first thought that pops into your mind before you enter a restaurant to meet someone for the first time? Your thought may be telling you to run, or it may be whispering softly that you should brace yourself for whatever comes. What do you think before entering a job interview? Perhaps you feel like you've got this, or maybe you're thinking about how many things could go wrong. You're even playing memories in your mind of the times you messed up, irrespective of the fact that these memories have nothing to do with this situation. Your inner critic is reminding you about how you fell off the monkey bars at school, and all the kids laughed at you and mocked you. Suddenly, you go white as snow as the elevator door opens to your interview.

What thought crosses your mind when you're about to purchase a car? Do you imagine yourself driving with a smile across your face because you're proud, or are you haunted by an endless stream of questions? What if I miss the payments? What if the car gets stolen? What if Sam buys a newer, fancier car? Think about what thought will pop into your mind if a friend tells you to share your incredible new product. Perhaps you're excited and can't wait to show it off to some investors, but maybe you're starting to question whether the product is of any use. Besides, you're not sure your friend is being honest. He might be blowing smoke up your backside just because he's your friend. Negative thinking is automatic and more common than positive thoughts.

Being pessimistic is when you have a pattern of negative thoughts about or toward yourself or your environment. Thoughts provoke your emotional and behavioral responses, so doubting yourself would make you feel fearful of trying while it shows in your behaviors when you become indecisive or make a decision you regret later. Everything you do and feel is based on what you think. It's dependent on what you believe and think about yourself, so negative thinking is responsible for much of your negative behavior. Everyone feels a little negative from time to time, but excessive negative thoughts can harm your mental health or be a sign of mental disorders. Negative thinking is a common symptom of depression, personality disorders, anxiety disorders, and schizophrenia (Smith & Croft, 2019).

However, negative thinking isn't a diagnosis-worthy sign that you have a mental disorder, but incessant pessimism can still have vast impacts on your life as you learned in Chapter One. Negative thoughts work on two main premises.

The first premise is that it will disqualify the positive side. You'll find yourself dismissing any positive aspects and focusing on the negative side, even though recognizing the positives may be far more rational. For example, you may make a mistake with a project at work, and that's all you can focus on, irrespective of the lessons you learned while correcting the mistake. You can only think about the time wasted while you fixed the problem you caused. The logical positive side of this scenario is that you learned something new. You wouldn't make the same mistake because you learned how to correct it, so focusing on self-blame and doubt is irrational. Only being able to focus on the negative side may also leave you thinking you'll always make the mistake, again and again.

The second premise of negative thoughts is that they'll either maximize or minimize the aspects within the experience. The negative aspects will be exaggerated while the positive factors are undermined. For example, someone pays you a compliment by saying, "Wow, that color shirt looks incredible, and so much more than the regular blue shirt." What you choose to think about is how this person said your blue shirts were boring and lame. How dare they say such a thing? You don't realize that they're telling you how wonderful white looks against your complexion. Maybe their words weren't clear enough, but that doesn't change the fact that your focus leans toward the negative undertone, which isn't always rational. It's not rational in this case.

Negative thinking is widely based on fear and trepidation, and you now know what designs them. You may fear the unknown, which is probably the most common fear in humans. Perhaps you fear the inability to cope with a situation, and your thoughts are wildly taken over by your inner demon, much like them being possessed. You may fear failure, or you can be nervous about the outcome of something that could change your life, such as a job interview. Fear is an incredibly powerful emotion, and it can put either the inner critic or the rational inner voice in the driver's seat of your thoughts. It's fear that triggers your thoughts, irrespective of where the fear comes from. Your self-doubt might brew fear because you're uncertain of your abilities, or you may just fear something you haven't succeeded with before. Either way, it conjures negative thinking.

The problem with negative thoughts is that they just pop up without any effort. They're automatic, and that makes them hard to even recognize sometimes. Other characteristics of negative thoughts can also help you know what they look and sound like. An unhelpful thought that affects the way you behave can prevent you from achieving what you desire in life. Any thought that moves you three steps back from where you wish to be might be unhelpful. Your thoughts should carry you closer to your goals, even if it's with half a step. Thoughts being too believable can also be a sign that you're thinking negatively. A thought can always be questioned. If you can't question it, it might not be reasonable. Thoughts aren't facts, and you can't believe they are facts unless you question them.

Distorted thoughts are the most common type of negative thinking, and they're the kind that doesn't fit into the facts, even though you continue to think that way. A thought should always consider all the facts. Otherwise, it's just a perception. Intrusive thoughts are also negative, and they include any thought you haven't chosen but you experience them anyway. Intrusive thoughts could be violent or disturbing, and they may signal a mental health disorder, so have them checked out. Intrusive thoughts are complicated creatures, and they're commonly experienced in mental disorders, one of which is post-traumatic stress disorder (PTSD). In the case of PTSD, it can be hard to switch them off without help. Asking for help is not a sign of strength and not weakness. It's an admirable decision, which shows how much you value your well-being.

Anyway, this gives you a good idea of what negative thoughts may sound and look like. Be careful of those subtle ones that only make you feel slightly bad. If you're questioning whether a thought is healthy or not, chances are that it isn't healthy. Your mind is a beautiful place, and you don't want it filled with distorted or unhelpful thoughts. You want your thoughts to be your own. You want them to look and sound like something that helps you move closer to what you desire in life.

Distorted Prospects

The ways in which we can think negatively are vast, but they're certainly not valuable or reassuring. They won't help you progress toward your desires and goals. They won't help you achieve greater well-being and happiness. If anything, they'll move you further away from what you want. Automatic negative thoughts are also conveniently called ANTs. Psychology has identified over 20 distorted and negative thinking patterns (Cicetti, 2013). That makes many different ANTs, which can be just as counterproductive as having ants crawling around your mind.

All or nothing thoughts are distorted, and they're also commonly called black and white or polarized thinking. The world would be pretty boring if only black and white existed. What about the lines of gray and other colors between them? This type of distortion makes you think you're either awesome or terrible. You're either successful or a complete failure. You're either loved or hated. You're either perfect or completely flawed. Perfection is a myth, and everyone is beautifully flawed in their own way.

Always being right is not a good color on any thinking pattern. If you think you can never be wrong, you're already mistaken. This distortion makes you think that being wrong is a great failure. It's not an option, and you'll do anything within your power to win arguments. People who don't think they're wrong can find it hard to be social and committed in a relationship. They may also find it hard to work in teams, and their employers won't be impressed with their perceived arrogance.

Blaming thoughts toward yourself or other people are also distorted. Self-blame is a distorted belief designed through experiences. You may blame yourself for everything that goes wrong. You might blame yourself for a traumatic event that was out of your control. However, you may also blame others for your pain, thinking they could control what happened. Obviously, you'll blame an assailant for hurting you, but you can't blame your friend who didn't pick you up from work on time when she was stuck in traffic.

Catastrophizing is another ANT. An obsession with "what if" is a good sign you're experiencing catastrophic thought patterns. What if I did this differently? What if I controlled my temper toward my boss? What if the world ends tomorrow? Catastrophizing is a thought pattern where you think disaster is inevitable. You're quite certain that only the worst can happen.

Control fallacies are also distorted. A sense of false control over situations and outcomes can be detrimental to your mental health. Either you think everything bad happens only to you, claiming the title of a victim, or you feel like the burden is on your shoulders to make someone happy. Bad things happen to everyone, every day. You also must realize that you aren't responsible for someone else's happiness. We all pave our own roads. In some cases, you even think you need to make everyone happy. The control fallacy may make you think you have no control or too much of it.

Discounting the positive in your mind can also show distorted patterns. You'll recognize something good, and you may even receive recognition for what you did, but you won't accept it. You'll reject accomplishment and success as irrelevant experiences. You'll say that anyone can do it or that it doesn't count. You won employee of the month, but you brush it off as something anyone can achieve. Your partner proposes, and you think that it's not that phenomenal because it happens every day, irrespective of how he flew you to Hawaii to propose on the beach.

Emotional reasoning is also flawed as a thought. Emotions and logic can never be placed in the same boat. This distortion may have you thinking that emotional significance proves a fact. You think you're ugly, so you have to be. You think you're stupid, so it must be true. You think you're undateable, so who in their right mind will want you? Emotional reasoning designs a false reality, and it can stir endless self-doubt and low self-esteem.

Fairness fallacies are also ANTs. In this pattern of thought, you may think you're the only person who knows what is fair. You can't see and understand what others consider to be fair. You may also find it hard to accept other people's perspectives because they have no clue what fairness looks like according to you. Fairness is a delicate concept that should consider many factors and both sides of a story. You may also feel like you're constantly being treated unfairly if you have this distortion. It's another form of feeling like a victim, too.

Fallacies of change is another common ANT. The fallacy is that you think you can change the way people treat you, love you, and appreciate you. However, you can never control someone else's thoughts or feelings. You can't change people, just as they can't change you. You certainly can't change people's thoughts and feelings; otherwise, we'd have a world of like-minded people.

Filtering is another distortion. This is the thoughtful pattern of choosing one tiny aspect of a large picture and focusing on that, and it's always the negative aspect that gets chosen. It doesn't matter if your boss complimented 20 aspects of your work in your annual assessment. He also pointed out the fact that you don't smile enough. Your performance review was exceptional, but you choose to focus on the smile comment, which was merely a form of positive encouragement. Filtering is like focusing on the fly zooming around the Sistine Chapel.

Fortune telling is another cognitive distortion commonly experienced in negative thinking. You can't know what is to come. No one can. Otherwise, time travel would mentally be possible, but for now, there's no such thing. Anticipating undesirable outcomes, and thinking they're facts, is just another way you can use negative thinking to disturb your life.

Global labeling is the most extreme form of generalizing while you place exaggerated labels on people. These labels are loaded with emotions, making them irrational. You may label yourself or others. For example, you failed a quiz at school, so you automatically assume you'll always be the world's greatest idiot. You let something slip when talking to a friend, so you must be a lifetime backstabber. Sara disagreed with your perspective, so she must be a lifelong cow. That's what the extreme version of generalizing people does to your mind. You give yourself and others lifelong labels, driven by emotional significance. Other distorted labels may include words like 'never,' 'no one,' 'everyone,' 'everything,' 'every time,' and 'always.'

"Heaven's reward fallacy" is another known distortion. What is heaven? It's the place some of us think we'll end up if we live good lives that follow the rules. Thinking that rewards will come if you work hard and long enough is a recipe for disappointment. Rewards don't always follow a sacrifice. You're expecting to know the outcomes and what other people will do. You think your boss will promote you if you show grit and loyalty. The problem is that you can become bitter and angry when the reward doesn't come. People don't always do what we expect, and life doesn't always turn to the skies when we want it to.

Jumping to conclusions is often a subtler distorted thought. People may tell you to stop thinking before you know the facts. You interpret outcomes and experiences negatively, but you don't have the facts to prove their negativity. Perhaps your friend hasn't called for some time now, so you automatically think she hates you. Your boss didn't smile at you today, so he must be absolutely enraged by you. Your partner didn't reciprocate your "I love you" this morning, so she must be losing interest. Maybe she didn't hear you. Maybe your boss didn't see you, and perhaps your friend is dealing with a crisis.

Magnifying thoughts are also ANTS. You may exaggerate mistakes by ruminating on them and talking endlessly about them. You blow things out of proportion, even if someone reassures you that it wasn't so bad. Thinking your inability to meet a deadline would bring the apocalypse is a sign you're having negative thoughts. Magnification is also the negative thoughts that make you comparatively make someone else's achievement sound greater than it is. You may even focus on your mistakes and compare them to the accomplishment of someone else.

Mind reading can also be a sign of distorted thoughts. Making assumptions and negative interpretations of what other people think is a distortion. We are not a society of soothsayers and clairvoyants. No one can read another person's mind, and that's a good thing. Would you want people to know what goes on inside your mind? Our thoughts are precious and private, and we can't share them without moving our lips. The advantage of this is that we get to choose what we say. However, don't assume you can read someone's mind because you're probably reading it wrong anyway.

Minimizing is the opposite of magnifying. This is when you undermine your value and relevance. You start questioning your qualities and abilities. Before you know it, you're wondering why your partner chooses to stay with you. You're not good enough for them. They can do so much better than you. You're always comparing yourself to other people.

Negative rumination is another ANT. Self-reflection is healthy when you're practicing it for growth purposes, but thinking too long and hard about your past negative experiences will only keep your mind trapped in a pessimistic bubble. You may become depressed if you continue to focus intently on your mistakes, traumas, and undesirable experiences.

Outward-directed anger is also a distorted way of thinking. Everyone has been treated poorly by someone in their lives, even if it was a once-off experience. Our first impression of someone may also set the stage for us to generalize everyone who seems remotely similar to them, and we tend to hold a subtle grudge that shows in our interactions and thoughts toward these people. You can't begrudge someone you don't know, even if they remind you of someone who hurt you. Outward-directed anger is when you assume the worst of anyone who resembles a class of person you've generalized.

Overanalyzing is one of the ANTs you may easily recognize. It's logically a great way of approaching a problem by thinking thoroughly about what you should do next. This allows you to consider various options, but overthinking can become a problem when it stops you from making a decision. Taking too much time to consider options and obsessively overanalyzing every detail can indicate a distorted pattern of thought. It may lead to indecisiveness or procrastination, both of which aren't conducive to your growth.

Overgeneralization is also an ANT. Generalizing experiences can be the downfall of your mental health. It makes you expect the worst all the time, even if you're doing great. People who think this way will assume they'll fail every time because of one failure. They'll assume the vegetable garden will be a waste again because it was wasteful last year. These kinds of people will struggle to get back on the horse after falling off it.

Personalization is a distorted way of thinking and believing that everything is about you. Other people can't have their own thoughts without considering you. Your best friend started playing the piano at a bar on the other side of town. He must be doing this because he knows you won't go there. Your dad stopped watching the football on Sundays because you like to join him, and he doesn't want you around anymore. Your friend might be receiving more money on that side of town, and your dad might be attending church because he's been lonely since your mom died. He might be seeking company.

'Should' and 'must' thoughts are also distorted by nature. You can't tell people they should do this or that. You might have theories about how things should be done, but other people can have different perspectives and values. Having this distortion would make you think people must obey your way of living or completing a task. You think people should be this romantic in relationships and that intelligent in their conversations. Your 'shoulds' are guided by expectations, which were set by your experiences throughout life. Often, these expectations are faulty. You feel angry when someone breaks your expectations, and you experience guilty thoughts when you break them.

There are so many ways in which you can have distorted thoughts, and many of them can easily go unnoticed. You must start listening to those voices chattering in your mind. You have to start questioning what they say, especially the demon who holds you back. You must learn to recognize the voice of unreason, so you can bring the rational voice back to the frontline. Only once you do this, can you truly know that you're heading in the right direction.

Recognizing ANTs

ANTs are the first-responder thoughts that instantly pop into your mind when you experience something. It's an impulsive thought that travels faster than sound and light. They're normally ignited when you feel strongly about something. Treating negative thoughts isn't as simple as dressing a physical wound. They've probably been part of your daily life for many years, if not your entire life. Negative thoughts are so deeply embedded within your mind that it's complicated to reveal them. This makes it hard for you to distinguish the critical inner demon voices from your genuine observations and your sense of self. If you can recognize your ANTs as they happen, you can break them down into three factors to bring the conscious, logical mind back to your attention.

First, you have to analyze the situation that triggered your anxiety, which caused the negative thought to surface automatically. You can help your logical mind be part of understanding the trigger by asking yourself who, what, when, and where? What were you doing when it happened, and who was around? Where were you during the trigger situation, and when did it happen? Be as specific as you can to return your attention to the facts.

Second, dissect your mood during the event. Were you feeling irritated, angry, afraid, or guilty? Use one word to describe how you felt at that moment, and give it a percentage to understand the significance of your emotional response. Don't overthink the percentage. Just go with your gut feeling as you rate the intensity of your emotional reaction. This rating will help you recognize how much of your thought was influenced by the underlying mood.

Finally, describe the automatic thought that ran through your mind at that moment. This is the most essential part of your analysis. Be as descriptive as you can when you think about what your thoughts looked and sounded like at that time. Did you think you were dumb? Perhaps you saw an image of your teacher yelling at you while you thought this. Maybe you thought you were unlovable, and you saw images of your parents shunning you for your sister. Did you think you were alone in this world? Perhaps you saw yourself sitting home alone on a Friday night because you don't have meaningful friends. Listen carefully to hear if voices are telling you how to feel while your thoughts are running. Did you hear a paranoid voice? Perhaps you heard a self-aggrandizing voice saying, "They're jealous of you," or "No one cares about your potential."

By the time you've divided a thought into these three sections, you may already see why the thought is irrational. You may understand how your experiences as a child have influenced your automatic responses. Moreover, you've probably recognized the voice of the demon. Once you can do that, you can make changes to the way you think. You can't face an enemy until you identify it. You can't fight an invisible opponent, and you can't debate with someone who speaks under their voice so you can't hear them. What you can do now is create a thought-recording journal. Design one on your laptop or a piece of paper. Create three columns that represent the sections in which you need to break your automatic thoughts, and start recording them as they come. It might take some time to see patterns between the thoughts. Don't expect yourself to identify your distortions after one entry.

Continue journaling your thoughts and breaking them into three sections until you recognize regular patterns. Remember that everyone has a negative thought once in a while, so patterns are your target. Then, you can go through the list of cognitive distortions to see which patterns you may use. Not only are you identifying the thoughts, but you're also recognizing triggers, which is ultimately useful if you want to reduce your exposure to them. Once you find your list of triggers, you can know which situations need improvement or reduction. Your triggers might include speaking up in a meeting, attending social events, or asking someone on a date. They could also include taking on a new work project, telling your partner how you feel about them, or accepting a call from your parents who may not have been the most supportive in your childhood.

Knowing the moods that lead to the responses in your thoughts can also help you understand what your emotional insecurities are and how to deal with them. Anxiety, fear, shame, guilt, irritability, or doubt can show you what needs some work. We all have emotional insecurities embedded into our primitive minds. Some people are more afraid of shame, and others are terrified of anything that makes them fearful in the first place. We also can't avoid every scenario that triggers us, so changing our automatic thoughts might be the best way to gradually overcome insecurity. At the end of the day, recording your automatic behavior and thoughts can help you identify how you attack yourself. Then, you'll be better equipped to manage and change the ANTs. You'll be able to silence the voice of the demon and listen more attentively to the logical mind.

Learn to identify and doubt your thoughts because that's the first step to regain control of your emotional and behavioral responses. What is the voice of the demon saying to you? Now, how can you change it?

Chapter 4:

Fighting off the Demons

What do priests do with demons who possess a human? They exorcise them in these elaborate movies that end in sleepless nights. Well, the great news is that your inner demons are not the same kind as those seen in horror movies. However, you want to take control of the critters running amok. You want to corner them in some cases, and you may want to just give them a little attention in other moments. You can do just that now that you know how they look and sound. There's no place for them to hide anymore. It's time to fight your negative thoughts to embrace a better quality of life.

A Fundamental Change

When negative thoughts come as they will, and you identify them for what they are, there are numerous ways to deal with them to prevent them from getting stuck in your mind. Different strategies will benefit different people, so keep experimenting with techniques until you find one that works. Think about thoughts this way. They can often behave similarly to toddlers.

Every toddler reacts differently to their parents. You're a parent to the little demon critters in your mind. Some strategies you test may scare them off, but others may turn them into those kinds of toddlers that bite you. Mostly, the strategies that don't work for you will be like the toddler who adamantly ignores their parents. What do you do with toddlers? You set boundaries and remain consistent as a parent. You can't be consistent until you find your working strategy, but once found, keep it active.

Negative thoughts require one boundary that isn't negotiable. You should have a zero-tolerance policy for unruly behavior, namely rumination. Don't give attention to a thought that encourages you to ruminate on it. You'll be losing this battle if you allow it to take root in your mind. A systematic review was published in *Clinical Psychology Review*, which included 19 studies (Querstret & Cropley, 2013). The purpose of the review was to determine which techniques have significantly reduced rumination over 10 years. Mindfulness and cognitive-behavioral therapy (CBT) were the two main assets that changed the likelihood of rumination in people with depression and anxiety. Mindfulness teaches you to be aware of your mind and body in the present moment without judgment, and CBT also encourages increased awareness of how thoughts interact with emotions and behaviors.

Adopting a zero-tolerance boundary with your thoughts means you'll be aware of them, but you'll take action to encourage different thoughts and behaviors. It takes practice, but you need to acknowledge your thoughts and emotions. They won't go away on their own if you ignore them. However, you won't spend attention on rumination, which only allows the thought and accompanying emotion to behave poorly. This crosses your zero-tolerance boundary for rumination, which is the single behavior you won't allow the toddler to express. Embrace the thought once you notice it because this absorbs far less mental energy than ignoring it. You don't need to always forcibly fight back. Sometimes, there's a hidden truth behind negative thinking. What it shows you is that the situation matters a lot to you. Otherwise, it wouldn't ignite your emotions enough to react this way.

What you may find is that some thoughts will dissipate on their own if you embrace them and step back. You're giving it attention, but only on your terms. This might be enough for some negative thoughts. Being aware of your negative thoughts, embracing them with your zero-tolerance boundary, and stepping away from them can help you accept that you're not your thoughts. Your thoughts don't define you in any way. They're a part of you. They reflect an experience, but they don't define what comes next. Thoughts don't seem as serious anymore once you separate yourself from them. Separate your identity from the inner voice that urges you to focus on your negative thoughts. Diffuse the bomb inside your mind by staring at it and having enough control to follow your zero-tolerance boundary.

Keep in mind that thoughts and reality are two separate entities. Your thoughts can be as flawed as anyone else's. After all, they're exposed to the same biases and emotional influences every person experiences. Your inner critic can be as tainted as the next, or it may be as silent as a mouse. That's in your hands now. It will take time. Remember that negative thinking is an addiction, so be gentle with yourself as long as you keep your boundary in place. There's one strategy many people use to silence their inner critic when it starts blurting out doubts and hesitations. You can intercept most negative thoughts by asking yourself five questions when they pop into your mind.

First, is the thought in any way true or realistic? Recognize whether the thought has any foundation of reality. If not, it can't be true. Thoughts without evidence are as pointless as the rain watering the ocean. Answering this question already reminds you that your inner voice doesn't always speak in facts or truthfully.

Second, is the thought empowering you in any way, or do you feel like the thought is taking power away from you? Perhaps the thought makes you feel better able to cope with the situation. If it doesn't, then it's taking your power away. Either way, it influences your behaviors. An empowering thought might motivate you, but one that removes your power can leave you struggling to cope with the situation.

Third, is there a way for you to spin it into a positive thought or lesson? Consider whether this thought teaches you something new. Maybe your first cake was a complete flop, and this triggered a thought to remind you about your lack of intelligence. Messing up a baking recipe doesn't mean you're stupid. It means you need to check the recipe again and see if you can do something differently. Upon investigation, you see that you missed baking soda, so your second cake comes out fantastic. You're able to learn something new each day, and sometimes, negative thoughts can be spun into positive outcomes.

Four, what would life look and be like for you if the inner critic wasn't saying this? Ponder on the options of where you will be right now if the thought didn't interrupt your experience. In the long run, persistent thought patterns may be holding you back from becoming a leading entrepreneur or the best executive in the city. It might be preventing you from moving forward in relationships.

Finally, is the thought masking an underlying issue that needs to be addressed? Perhaps you're thinking that you'll look like a fool if you jump off the bridge. No rule says you have to jump, and your thought might simply be reminding you of your fear of heights. This doesn't mean you should change the thought. It indicates an underlying fear or hesitation you may have to deal with.

If these five questions don't help you take back control of the negative thought, you can ask yourself what you really desire, how you can make the best of the situation, or whether there's anything else you can think about instead. Your inner critic and thoughts are designing your narrative. Do you want a demon-child to write your life story, or do you want to write it yourself? You can only be authentic if you write it yourself. Set your boundary on zero rumination, and ask yourself questions that make you see a different perspective, and then you'll have the fundamental strategy to change your inner narrative. However, there are many more strategies from which you can benefit.

Stop Negative Self-Talk

Hush the demon-child before it creates an uninviting environment in your mind. The inner critic can be our worst enemy, but we can do something about it. Pay attention to what it has to say by listening to your thoughts. Pay special attention when you hear your inner critic talking to you in a way you wouldn't repeat. Your inner voices should speak to you as a good friend or child, and be careful about what you say back to the inner critic. Would you tell a child that they're stupid? Would you tell a friend that they're fat? Would you tell your brother that he can't do anything right? No, you wouldn't. You shouldn't allow the inner critic to speak to you like this, either. There are ways to stop it from speaking like this.

You can start by giving the inner critic a nickname. By giving it a goofy nickname like demon-child, showboat, braggart, or Ally Ross, you will separate your inner critic from yourself. You'll start seeing it as an external force that doesn't define you. This makes your inner critic easier to recognize, and you don't have to agree with it. Imagine calling your inner critic a demon-child. A demon is an unlovable creature, and a child is just another tantrum waiting to happen, so the name suits the inner critic. You'll start seeing the ridiculousness of what it speaks.

Another way to tone down the criticism is by challenging the inner critic. The reason it became so loud is probably due to you not challenging it. The inner critic is quite sensitive in that sense. It doesn't expect a challenge, so it might be surprised enough to shut up. Cross-examine your inner critic, especially when you realize how exaggerated the thought is. Your inner critic might say, "Wow, you're going to mess this relationship up." Stop it, call it out by its chosen nickname, and counter its thoughts. "I'm going to make the best of this relationship." Maybe your inner critic says, "You're a total loser." Start toning down the response to challenge the inner critic. You can say, "I'm willing to improve and grow my skills." It might not listen at first if you're toning your challenges down too much, but you'll notice how the inner critic slowly becomes weaker.

Sometimes, it can be difficult to stop a running thought while it's moving at the speed it does. This is when you can change the intensity of what it says instead. Perpetually introduce the inner critic to gentler language. When it says, "I hate this!" you can say, "I don't like this much." You can start slowly downgrading this to saying, "I don't prefer this method." Downplaying the inner critic's language can take its power away.

Saying a thought out loud can also startle an inner critic. Think for a moment about a thought you wouldn't easily share with a good friend. Why won't you do this? Chances are that you wouldn't say it out loud because you're afraid of how it will sound. The other possibility is that it may be absolutely ridiculous. Try telling a good friend what's on your mind when your inner critic speaks up again. Allow the laughter to silence its voice. Otherwise, you can also say it out loud when you're alone. You might experience the same response when you hear how ridiculous it sounds. Hearing the words outside of our thoughts can help us recognize whether they sound realistic or not. This can shine a rational spotlight on the inner critic.

Finally, you can also use an intentional stop sign to prevent the train of thought from progressing. You can visualize a stop sign if you hear the inner critic talking away, or you can counter it with a random thought that makes no sense. Who knows? You might get a giggle out of demon-child. Your inner critic might say, "Wow, this day will be my end." You can randomly say, "Why is grass green and not blue?" The demon-child is highly sensitive to startling thoughts, so surprising it can hush it. You can also counter it with an alternative thought if it says, "You're not very attractive." You can say, "Wow, those guys couldn't take their eyes off me last week." Another way to use a figurative stop sign is by tying a rubber band around your wrist. Snap it every time your inner critic starts talking negatively.

These are ways to silence the chattering in your mind, but there are many ways to skin the same thought pattern. Some work faster if they work for you, and others take a little more time and practice.

Swift Battle Plans

Every general has two plans in his hand. He has a quick battle plan that could be implemented in the heat of the moment, and he has a plan for training his troops so they grow and improve over time. For now, you'll be learning about the fast strategies, some of which you can use daily and others you can use when you find yourself breaking your boundary. We all lean toward the negative side because of our addictions, so don't increase your self-blame if a negative thought pops into your mind. Take the bull by the horns, and set your plan in action to recommit to your boundary. These strategies will help you reduce the negative design in your brain, and they'll also gradually count toward your long-term training.

Contain your thoughts daily to reduce the amount of rumination you may experience. The reason it's so hard to catch a thought is that it travels at speeds you can't imagine. According to the Dent Neurologic Institute (2019), the human brain can process information at speeds between 150 and 250 miles per second. The speed of light is only roughly 186 miles per second. That makes it hard to catch every thought. Your brain is so active that it could power a lightbulb. It also uses 20% of your energy, which is sourced from glucose.

Now, how can you capture negative thoughts if they travel at these speeds, especially in the subconscious mind?

Quite frankly, you can't catch each one, but you can contain your negative thoughts by dedicating rumination slots in your daily planner. The negative thoughts trying to disrupt your day can be allocated to half an hour of pondering daily. This leaves enough time to think about your options but set a timer to ensure you aren't getting carried away. Also, only allow it to criticize certain things during this time. Don't give attention to thoughts that break your self-worth. Rather dedicate this time to thoughts that may bring lessons or answers.

Another way to change negative thoughts is by expressing them on paper, according to psychiatrist David Burns (Woolston, 2019). Seeing your thoughts on paper can help you investigate them logically and compare them to the distorted list in the previous chapter. Then, you can think about a rational rebuttal or alternative thought, which you can also write down. Writing your thoughts allows you to regain power over them. You separate them from yourself again. You can also crumple or burn the paper when you're done. You're freeing yourself from the thought as the paper burns. You'll already regain some control simply by writing it and crumpling the paper. Imagine the thought running down your arm and into your hands as it exits your mind through the pen. Writing, burning, crumbling, or challenging the thought on paper can teach your mind to reject it.

A great way to silence the negative thoughts in the moment is to pretend like you're a best friend talking to someone who thinks poorly about themselves. Sit in a quiet place while you talk to yourself in front of a mirror. Tell the person in the mirror what you think of them. Let them know that they're good, smart, attractive, and intelligent enough. Speak to them as you would talk to the person you love most in this world.

Distraction is also commonly a good cure for sudden negative thoughts, and it's great for your mental well-being when you halt rumination to think about something entirely different. It's also a compassionate way for you to manage your thoughts when they turn negative. Distraction is a good tool when you find yourself breaking your rumination boundary again. Find something else to think about. Challenge your brain with a Sudoku puzzle, or read a book. You can also go for a walk, watch a funny video on YouTube, or call a friend to talk about anything else that doesn't fixate your attention on a negative thought.

Ask your friend what's new in their lives, and make plans for the weekend. Plan fun activities that move your mind far away from that which troubles you. Go on a hiking trip, or have coffee with your best friend. Any movie, book, or activity you choose to do should be fast enough to take your mind off things, and they should be positive, so don't watch horror movies and dramas that make you feel worse. That will only bring back rumination. Feed your mind with laughter, happy moments, and great memories to compassionately soothe negative thoughts. Challenging your mind with puzzles will wake the logical mind up to stop negative thinking.

Another way to start proving your negative thoughts wrong is to take action before you can think twice. This is a good way to show your mind how wrong it is when it says things like "you can't do this" or "you're boring." Commit to working on a project for two minutes at a time until your mind realizes you can do this. Strike up a conversation with a friend when it says you're boring. Invite a friend to lunch when your mind says you'll always be alone.

Ask someone on a date when it says you're not good enough. Apply for a senior promotion when your mind tries to make you believe you're leaping too far. Learn one new random fact when your mind says you're not intelligent enough. The internet is full of fun facts you can learn at the swipe of a screen. It doesn't matter what your mind challenges you with; you can take action. Behave in a way it won't expect. Take action against thoughts that aren't accurate or those that make you feel less worthy. This will move you closer to your authentic self, and your mind will start learning that you can do this.

Between startling your negative thinking patterns and showing it how wrong it perceives the world, you can make changes with time. Our thoughts are often wrong, or they have no evidence to justify what they say. Remember that your thoughts and inner critic are like a child. They need to be coached compassionately and gradually to learn what you want to start thinking. These tools will be your swift, actionable battle plans.

Training Plans

The general must train his troops now. Your conscious mind is the general in your brain, and it's the logical side of your mind that will slowly teach your troop thoughts how to best progress toward a desirable outcome. Keep in mind that you can't control outcomes, but you can come as close to your result as possible if you're always moving in the same direction. The last thing you want to do is move backward or remain stagnant. In life, we all want to be healthy, successful, happy, and grow into our better selves. There are a few ways you can train yourself to stop ruminating and giving the demon-child unwanted attention.

A change in perspective can work to maintain your zero-tolerance boundary for rumination, but it may take practice and time. Our perspectives have been set in place all our lives, so be patient with this one. Changing your perspective from the present to the future can be beneficial. You can't live in different timelines, but you can have goals and ambitions. Sometimes, looking at yourself two or five years from now can show you how insignificant the problem is at this moment. Will this problem still be there in another five years? Will it still matter? For example, maybe you're worried about your lack of abilities or experience at work. Understandably, you only started at the company three weeks ago. You might be expecting too much too soon. Will this fear still exist in two years, or will you learn how to do your work with finesse?

Maybe you're upset about something someone said to you this morning. They paid you a compliment with a negative undertone. Do you think this will still bother you in five years? If not, then you've successfully reduced the emphasis on your emotions, meaning the rumination can stop. You can also shift your perspective by imagining seeing the world from space. See yourself as a tiny speck on this huge globe beneath you. Your worries can't be as big as you think if you're so small compared to the world. You can also change your perspective by stepping outside of your situation. Imagine yourself as a spectator while you watch things pan out in your situation. Watch your problems from a distance, and just imagine for a moment that everything works out well. Who knows? Things might work out well.

You can also start reframing the way you see negative events. Perhaps you interpreted the situation as a negative experience, so you need to step back once more and focus on finding any positive side to the story. Let's say you walked into a room with investors, and they turned your product down. Your heart yearns to become an entrepreneur, and this rightfully shatters you. The only thing you can think about is how they weren't prepared to invest in your product. You invented a gadget that tracks cats in real-time. It goes on their collars, and their owners can find them when they go on a walkabout. You did two things right. You researched a demand, and you created a product to fill it. The investors were impressed, and they were asking you endless questions. This is where you fell short, so think harder about the questions they asked. They wanted to know about marketing, production, and estimated returns on their investments.

You never had information for any of their most pressing questions. This is when their demeanor changed, and you were booted from the room. See it from their perspective. They need to know the details behind the amazing invention. They didn't become wealthy through blind investments. This is in no way a negative situation, either. The investors have taught you about what needs to be done first. Once you have a business plan, you'll most likely get an investor on board when you return. Throwing the product away, and thinking you're a complete failure is what you shouldn't ruminate on. You should work on a plan that would hook the investors. Reframing your thoughts doesn't mean you must wear rose-colored glasses. You must be realistic, too. You also won't ignore danger, but you'll give an equal significance to negative and positive aspects.

Changing your thought patterns isn't forcible. It should be a gradual shift from pessimism to optimism, which takes time. You want to start replacing your negative thoughts with something better. Replacing them with something the mind prefers with practice is far more likely to work than forcing your mind to think positively. What happens when you force an addict to stop using narcotics? They can suffer from withdrawal symptoms, and they need to be supervised. Your mind will attempt to return to its habits, so gentle changes are essential. Start taking small steps toward thinking about better things.

Positive replacement thoughts can also give you a sense of accomplishment. Your brain may release the feel-good chemicals that encourage the mind to prefer these thoughts. You just have to repeat them until your patterns change out of preference. When you find yourself thinking negatively again, be kind to yourself. Take a step back first, and allow yourself to just acknowledge the thought without ruminating on it. When you manage to step toward positivity, savor the moment. Savor the experience and all the wonderful aspects you can enjoy. Be present in positive experiences so your brain stores the information in long-term memory.

Start establishing new patterns in your thoughts. Remember to distract your mind with something more positive when you feel rumination lurking nearby. You need to repeat an activity to create a habit. Look for a new hobby you can do at home for those times you worry about something in the future. Keep your mind creatively busy with painting, playing an instrument, or working in the garden. Sometimes, your mind just needs a rest before it can think clearly about the future. Have a go-to hobby that gives your mind the rest it needs. Hobbies can also help you stay focused on your strengths. We tend to choose hobbies that align with our greatest skills, which can create a regular positive experience when you need a temporary escape from your thoughts.

If you reach a stage where your thoughts are seriously impacting your daily life and your functional abilities, it might be time to seek help from a professional. Negative thoughts are normal in everyone's life, but you might need expert guidance if it's sucking all the joy out of your life. Other symptoms that head caution and signal professional guidance are depression, mania, suicidal thoughts, or hallucinations. Mania is an extreme and sudden fluctuation in your moods. You can either be extremely depressed or unexplainably excited. Hallucinations are the brain's way of signaling for help. They're caused by chemical changes in the brain, so they require expert care. Depression should also never be underestimated if you can't function normally, and suicidal thoughts must be the most extreme form of negative thinking.

You can call your local crisis center, primary physician, mental health agency, or 911. Counseling and therapy can help you navigate life's changes because the only thing we can be sure of is that life will change. Changes always come, and they bring a host of negative feelings and thoughts if you have underlying depression or anxiety. They can also cause anxiety and depression, so don't be brave if you think you need help. Therapy can also help you achieve personal growth and reduce emotional suffering. Protecting your mind is an essential part of living a good quality of life, which you'll learn more about in the next chapter.

Chapter 5:

Protecting Your Mind

A hint of nostalgia, a dash of optimism, and a pinch of hope is a recipe to protect the mind. What goes into the mind will always be like seeds incepting the future. These seeds haven't borne fruit before, but changing the recipe, even on the smallest scale, can already begin to plant seeds that will bear fruit. Your mind can be a wonderful place, one you don't have to fear. You can keep negative thinking at bay by establishing habits that counter automatic negative thoughts.

Secrets to a Beautiful Mind

A beautiful mind can see all sides of a story, which means you must see the negative and positive sides. You won't be ruminating on the negative side with your zero-tolerance boundary, but you also need to *train your mind for positive acknowledgment*. Being able to see the silver linings can certainly protect your mind when negative events occur. Unfortunately, life isn't positive all of the time, so we need to have our minds ready for any scenario. We must become resilient against the potential negatives we may encounter. There are numerous ways you can become resilient against life.

The first thing to practice is to remove the words 'should' and 'must' from your language. This makes your mind more conducive to positive thought. The word 'should' is distorted. Saying you should be better at your work means you still think you're not good enough. 'Should' statements only make you anxious because they also sometimes demand the impossible. Start replacing these thoughts with flexible but concrete ones. Stop saying you should be more positive, and rather say you *can* be more positive by practicing meditation or cognitive restructuring. Stop leading your narrative with "I should." Rewire your self-statements and expectations by replacing 'should' words.

Instead of saying, "I should exercise daily," rather say, "I'll do my best to finish my workout daily."

Instead of saying, "I should stop always being so negative," rather say, "I plan to start seeing the positive side of things."

Instead of saying, "I should be able to meet someone new without fleeing from the restaurant," rather say, "I'll try my best to enjoy the company of this new person."

Instead of saying, "I should feel better about myself," rather say, "I'll try to value myself more each day."

Instead of saying, "I should be an expert with my work," rather say, "I'll improve my skills by learning something new every day."

Changing your verbal language isn't the only new habit you need. Tonality includes body language. Negative body language sends the wrong message to your brain. Imagine talking to someone, and they're smiling from ear to ear as they share bad news. Would you believe them? Improper body language can reduce your self-esteem and confidence, and it influences your emotional state. You're more likely to experience negative thoughts when you're emotional. You're being negative if you're hunched over your desk as you try to convince yourself how much better you'll do today. Sitting with better posture and a smile convinces your brain to feel better. Smile more, have an open posture, and walk tall.

Mental shopping is another way to make you smile. Think of anything you look forward to. Perhaps it's a product you can't wait to buy. Imagine yourself walking into Costco, Walmart, or wherever to purchase the item. Maybe you're waiting for the new release from your favorite author or a new album from your favorite musician. Maybe you want to mentally shop for a new pair of sneakers that brings you joy. What matters is that the item must mean a lot to you. Negative thoughts often pop into our minds when we're not doing anything, so giving your brain a meaningful workout can distract it with an alternative emotion.

Another method people with beautiful minds practice is to surround themselves with the kind of people who encourage optimism. You must detach yourself from negative people who have nothing better to do than share pessimism. Gossip is another negative trait because people focus on other people's shortcomings to hide their own. Negativity is a contagious disease, which can be compared to the coronavirus. What people say designs your experiences and perceptions, and you don't need that. When you surround yourself with positive and hard-working people, you'll automatically want to be more positive. Surrounding yourself with negative people will make you carry their burden.

Be careful of the media that ignites your perceptions of the world, too. Social media is the new norm of socializing, and it has the same influence over you. Television has long been a mood changer, especially the news, which is so exaggerated half the time that it turns a happy person into an anxious one. News channels focus on the negative side of everything. They don't often share stories of how someone beat the odds. They don't tell you how some guy kicked the fertility out of a criminal. Instead, they tell you about the poor criminal who can't have kids anymore. Social media is just as bad because we have to live up to the expectations of fake people. Now, we have filters so everyone can falsely make themselves as beautiful as they want, and everyone is wealthy. The problem is that people only post what glorifies them.

They don't post the regular stuff, but we still compare ourselves to them. Why don't we have five cars and three houses? Well, what we don't know is that this woman caught her husband cheating, and she took him for everything he had. We only see what people share, and they'll only share what they want us to see. Just as your childhood and your experiences throughout life have shaped your mind, so does the media. Social media is a society that sets unrealistic expectations and makes us think we're less than perfect. It started long before social media when magazines and newspapers designed what we 'should' look like. It designed what success 'should' look like. However, notice how the word 'should' sneaks back into your life with the media. Stay away from negative media if you want to design a beautifully authentic mind.

Judgment is another powerful subconscious trait we all possess to some extent, but letting go of it can enhance your positive mindset. It may not be easy to let it go, but it's possible. You'll feel peaceful and confident in your skin once you release your judgment toward yourself and others. You'll have to shift your judgment by consciously noticing it, allowing it to be what it is without trying to change it, and then allowing it to freely release itself. This takes practice, but you can do it! Judgment is another thought that needs to be recognized before it diminishes. You can also change your judgments to positive ones when you find yourself criticizing someone else, yourself, or a situation.

Let's say you're criticizing yourself for not being fast enough to type 1,000 words in half an hour. Firstly, take it from me, this will change with time. Secondly, you can shift your focus to a positive quality within your writing. Think about your creativity. Let's say you're judging someone else for being too talkative. Rather judge their good qualities by saying, "They have a good general knowledge." Judging an event can change from "this is a mess" to "this has taught me a valuable lesson to help me improve my approach." Practice considering an entire scenario, person, or yourself. Don't give in to the first judgment that drops into your mind.

We all tend to focus on our worst traits. We can't write fast enough, we can't solve the problem at work, or we can't make small talk on a first date. Other than preventing yourself from judging your worst qualities, start focusing on what makes you unique and valuable. Everyone has value in this world. What I might do well, you might not. However, you have skills I don't possess. You need to start focusing on your unique strengths. They're the wonderful qualities that help you bounce back from mistakes. Once you can bounce back from making mistakes, you'll be able to embrace the direction your life is intended to take. You'll feel more positive when you can dwell on your strengths instead of your weaknesses. The world would be full of perfect individuals who need no improvement if everyone only had strengths. That's an illusion.

And if your mind is still not as beautiful as you desire, you can turn negative thinking into a creative passion. Some of the world's greatest artists have used suffering to express themselves in incredible artworks. Art is a way of processing your emotions to help you release them. Be more creative with your negative emotions to prevent them from spilling into your thoughts. Paint a picture with the colors that express your emotions. Write a song that releases all the negative expressions. Draw something that makes you think "wow, my thoughts look good on paper." Being creative can break the habitual dynamic of your thoughts. You'll also more easily understand and control them. Creativity requires your brain to work rationally.

Beautiful minds can create unfathomable artworks, and you don't need to be Pablo Picasso. People love looking at art that makes them think. The days of traditional art are over. It's now time to create something that stirs thoughts and emotions, so don't be anxious to try. It would be interesting to create one picture and save it for five years. Then, you can observe it and try to recognize what you thought at that moment. Chances are you won't easily be able to decipher it.

Three Foundational Practices

Three fundamental practices make your mind resilient toward negative thinking. Not only do they enable you to bounce back from negative thoughts when they occur, they also start exercising your mind like a muscle. You need to train your brain if you want to strengthen it.

The first exercise for your brain is meditation. Meditation allows you to clear your mind of negative thoughts and emotions while it reduces stress. Your mind will grow stronger, allowing you to untangle unwanted thoughts. You'll learn to let go of thoughts more easily, and you'll be kinder to yourself as meditation encourages non-judgment. You'll also gain a deeper sense of awareness. Meditation is a mindful practice, and mindfulness teaches you to increase your awareness of thoughts and emotions without trying to judge them. You must be present to be aware of what's happening right now. This makes your efforts much stronger because repressing emotions and thoughts will only backfire.

Research published in the *Annual Review of Psychology* has proven that thought suppression is harmful to your resilience and mental strength (Wenzlaff & Wegner, 2000). Thoughts can't be suppressed and avoided to feel better because it's a temporary fix. These thoughts will bubble and explode when you least want them to. You can't make a thought, memory, or emotion disappear by pretending it's not there. Mindfulness meditation will help you uncover the thoughts; give them enough attention without judgment, and you'll recognize how the thoughts become insignificant the longer you leave them alone. Tough love isn't always the answer, especially with negative thinking.

Meditating to enhance your awareness and release negative thoughts will strengthen the mental capacity you have for them. This should be a daily practice. Do it in the mornings if you're anxious about the day, or meditate at night if you want to release ruminating thoughts about mistakes you might've made during the day. Mindfulness meditation is best achieved in a quiet place where you're alone with your thoughts. You must be comfortable and your eyes must be shut, and then you can follow these three steps.

Step one is to start drawing a breath deep into your belly. You should feel your stomach rise and your chest remain still. Breathe into the belly with a long and even breath as you count to three, and then hold it there for three seconds before you press the air out for another three counts. Try to draw breath through the nose and express it through your mouth.

Step two is for when you feel calmer and more present in the awareness of what's happening in your body. Now, shift your focus to the negative thought. Don't judge or change it. Just pay attention to how you feel while your mind thinks this way. Continue breathing evenly for a few moments.

The third step is to allow the thought to release itself from your mind. Breathing in brings positive calmness to your mind, but breathing out slowly deletes the thought. Imagine seeing your negative thought as a pixelated image. The air flowing out of your mouth is chipping away pixel by pixel. As the image fades, allow yourself to take one deep and powerful breath before you slowly release it. You should feel calmer after this.

Try to practice meditation at least once daily. You'll start feeling a greater sense of control over your thoughts and emotions. Once you're experienced with mindful control, you can assert yourself over thoughts when they occur.

Forgiveness is the second practice to strengthen your mind. The act of forgiveness was reviewed by the University of Minnesota, and it proved to be an effective improvement for mental, physical, and emotional well-being (Lawson, 2012). Forgiveness doesn't only feel good when your heart releases pain and anger toward yourself or others. It also improves your immune system when you're not holding onto hurtful emotions and thoughts. The review also exposed the connection between forgiveness and longevity, meaning you'll live longer if you don't hold onto negativity. Your blood pressure and cardiovascular health also improve as you learn to forgive.

Forgiveness simply means you release your negative thoughts and feelings surrounding an event, even though it was negative. Maybe a friend insulted your intelligence by offering help with a problem. Your friend has offered assistance, so you can see this as a positive experience. You can't hold onto anger and frustration because your friend found a solution you didn't consider. Take a more significant example. You were involved in a car accident that hurt someone. Hating yourself for what happened won't change the past. You must forgive yourself to relinquish the pain you feel because it conjures negative emotions. You're likely blaming yourself for something you had no control over. Let's say your partner cheated on you. This is a tough one, but it must be forgiven. You'll be the person who suffers from rumination and self-defeating thoughts if you don't forgive your partner. Forgiveness doesn't mean you forget. It means you choose to let go of the feelings and thoughts that only hurt you. Learn to forgive, and your mind will be yours again.

Gratitude is the third mental workout to practice daily. The University of California conducted two studies related to gratitude among students who suffered from depression and anxiety (Brown & Wong, 2017). The first study divided students who were about to receive counseling into three groups. The first group only received counseling, the second group had to write about their negative experiences daily, and the third group had to write a gratitude letter to one person per week for three weeks. Not surprisingly, the gratitude group showed significant improvements in their mental health compared to the other two groups.

The second study included the same groups of students, but the university used functional magnetic resonance imaging (fMRI) to scan their brains. The gratitude group showed improved functions in the medial prefrontal cortex, which is connected to logical thoughts. The students also showed distinct differences from the other students who were still experiencing guilt and rumination. The scans were taken three months after the first study began, proving that gratitude has long-term benefits. Gratitude is when you acknowledge and appreciate the positive aspects of life, people, and experiences. This has a powerful effect on your emotional well-being. If you can find reasons to be grateful, even while your life might be challenging, you're on your way to a stronger, positive mind. You don't have to be grateful for huge things, like getting a promotion or meeting someone incredible. You can break a bigger gratitude into 50 aspects.

A promotion means you're thankful for having the skills required to do your job. You're grateful for the chance to grow, and you appreciate your boss who values you. You're grateful for the way your new partner smiles, and you can name 10 things you love about the way they talk. Noticing even the smallest of things you can be thankful for changes your quality of life. It's not the once-off promotion or meet-up that makes you happy. It's all the moments in each day that make you feel better. You're grateful for waking up healthy today. You're thankful for the compliment a random cashier gave you this morning. You appreciate the reminder from a friend to take next weekend off. The best way to practice gratitude is to keep a gratitude journal daily. Add five things daily. They can be experiences, people, and even something you did today. You'll find reasons to be grateful when you're looking for them.

These three practices move you closer to your optimistic mind without making you dread the change. Remember that baby steps are the best way forward, so practice these techniques once a day for five minutes if you must. Stretch your time gradually.

The Fourth Fundamental

There's one more fundamental practice to achieve a positive mindset. Your mind determines how your brain thinks about your life circumstances. Training your brain to think differently rewires the synapses between neurons, and it changes your brain's structure and functionality (Reynolds, 2011). You can reinforce the connections between the left prefrontal cortex and the limbic system to control your emotions. You can also stimulate the growth of new connections, neurons, and thought patterns. Your mental productivity and analytical thinking will improve, allowing you to solve problems faster and be more creative. Your perspective can change, and your attention will be regulated to ensure you're focusing on what matters.

Moreover, you'll be releasing feel-good chemicals like serotonin, which makes the brain prefer the new thought patterns. The more you demand from your brain, the more it creates cortical space to supply the demand. This way, you'll be able to handle more tasks. Repeating any focused mental activity of your choice enforces stronger connections where you desire, and it will weaken the connections from previous habits. All you must do is start thinking happy, positive thoughts and refocusing your attention when negativity comes. Taking action gives the brain motivation to continue. Motivation doesn't always come from desire. Action also ignites it. Start practicing actionable thought changes daily. Instead of thinking food is either good or bad, rather consider a balance. Have some dessert but cut something else out like starch.

Instead of thinking you can't do this, give yourself a chance to try by taking it one minute at a time. Instead of thinking your exercise routine is messed up by the rain, have an indoor workout. Instead of comparing yourself to your colleague when they finished work two hours early, remind yourself that you have more responsibilities. Instead of thinking you'll never solve a problem, try something new. Just be careful not to overwhelm yourself with positive emotions at first. It could reinforce feelings of failure and worthlessness when life doesn't pan out as you hoped. Unrelenting optimism can backfire. Prohibiting certain emotions is considered denial and repression. Remember that you're training your brain. You're not forcing it to think differently overnight.

Cognitive-behavioral therapy is based on the relationship between thoughts, emotions, and behaviors, so it's useful to train your brain. CBT commonly uses a few different techniques to achieve the desired changes. It helps you to outsmart negative thinking patterns without repressing them. CBT can successfully help you learn and recognize illogical thoughts, stop them, and replace them with accurate alternatives. You also learn to relax your mind and body and manage your time better, which reduces your stress levels. Moreover, you find peace with criticism because constructive criticism can be useful. CBT can be practiced on your own, or you can consult a psychologist who will guide you through the restructuring process and give you homework to start practicing CBT yourself.

Three CBT techniques can open your mind to optimism. Cognitive restructuring is the first technique, and it has five steps. Restructuring your thought patterns helps you replace the negative self-talk with positive, helpful alternatives. Whether you're doing this at home or in therapy, you need to go through all five of the steps. The steps help you identify, accurately evaluate, and replace the thought. You'll need a sheet with seven columns, or you can create an Excel spreadsheet. Each step will fill specific columns.

Step one is self-monitoring. This requires you to fill the first three columns. You'll have to identify the trigger situation that made you feel and think the way you did in the first column. The second column is where you write the automatic thought that popped into your mind, and the third column is to write your emotion when you thought the way you did. Rate your emotion on a scale of one to 10. Continue filling the first three columns until you see distorted patterns. It can also show you where your vulnerability lies.

Step two is to question your assumptions. This is where you'll fill column four, and possibly five. You'll have to answer a few questions to fill the fourth column:

- Is the thought emotional or factual?

- Is there evidence of the thought being true? This answer goes into column four.

- Is there evidence that the thought is untrue? This answer goes into column five.

- Could I test the thought?

- Is there another way for the information to be understood?

Step two has given you entries for the fourth column, and it will only give you an entry for the fifth column if the thought is factual. Otherwise, it already shows that the thought was a mere assumption. Then, you can move to step three.

Step three is to gather evidence. Now, you'll definitely fill column five. You want to question your beliefs, expectations, assumptions, feelings, thoughts, and trigger situations. You'll have to understand why you felt the way you did, where the belief comes from, and what evidence you can use against the original thought. You can write a pros and cons list for the belief that underlines the thought. Be specific about the details in the trigger situation and identify untruths ignited by fear or doubt.

Ask someone else to look at your facts for and against the thought before moving ahead. Let's say your thought was triggered by a smirky boss after you delivered your presentation. Your thought was that you messed up. The fifth column may have evidence against the thought now when you remind yourself of how many successful presentations you've already handed over. Your employers' smirk might've had nothing to do with you. Once you record your evidence against the automatic thought, you can move ahead.

Step four is to perform a cost-benefit analysis. What benefits do the current train of thought bring to your life? Does it improve the way you feel or not? Do you get anything out of thinking this way, or does it cost you attention and better well-being? Will it change your life if you didn't think this way? Is this thought advancing or limiting your performance at work? To continue with the presentation example, this thought would be a cost. It costs you attention, which could cost you lost time and work. The benefits of thinking this way don't exist because your original thought was an assumption.

Step five is to generate alternative thoughts, and it fills the last two columns. Once you know the pros and cons of your original thought, and you clarify the evidence in support or against it, you can consider an alternative thought. In this case, you can write down something like "It's unusual for my boss to act unprofessionally, but he has never given me a reason to fear him." Keep your alternative thought realistic and not too distant from the original one. Otherwise, the brain will reject it. Write your alternative thought in column six, and take a moment to realize how you feel before filling column seven. The final column is where you note the new rating between one and 10 for the emotion you wrote in column three. For example, you were anxious, rating it at eight. Now, you rate anxiety at two.

These five steps have also introduced the second technique you should be practicing daily. A thought record or journal is what the seven columns represent, and the longer you practice it, the more likely your thought patterns will change. It also helps you stay on top of the distorted patterns. Otherwise, you can keep a simple thought diary over a week or two to identify the patterns first. Write about your date that made you feel anxious. Record your physical reactions to the situation, and choose an alternative thought you can try next time. The trick is to try the alternative thought next time.

Finally, the third technique is about teaching you to assertively defend yourself against the inner critic. This exercise helps you cope with rejection and criticism from yourself and others. This technique is mostly taught in therapy to gradually grow your assertiveness, and your therapist will give you homework to further enhance it. You'll learn to have a pretend conversation to build assertive responses. You can do this at home though. You'll have to choose a few responses to the most common distortions you experience, especially those that criticize you. List 10 new statements you'll practice to respond with assertiveness, and then practice them in the mirror daily.

Remember not to make your responses too far from the original thoughts. You'll be toning them down gradually until you reach positive responses. When your common thought is that you're unattractive, respond by saying, "I don't like the way I look right now, but I'm working on improving that." Write yourself 10 responses you can practice for two weeks, and then use your thought diary to create 10 new ones. Shake it up to avoid your brain becoming bored. One thing you need to know is that disappointment also happens, so understand it may happen to you. You must accept disappointment, but keep your responses positive, or at least heading that way. Sometimes, we don't have control over the outcomes, and that can lead to disappointment, but that shouldn't bring you down.

What you need to learn is to love and accept yourself, and that will help you traverse the negativity that sneaks past your mental guards.

Chapter 6:

Accepting and Loving Yourself

Why is it so hard for us to love and accept the unique, authentic people we became? Negative thinking is deeply rooted in your childhood, especially if you grew up feeling unloved and underappreciated. Sadly, the people who instilled the lack of self-appreciation inside of you can't change the way you feel or think. Only you can do that! You can gradually shift the narrative in your mind to a more positive pattern by learning to love and be kind to yourself. It's the least you can do for yourself.

A Resistant Relationship

The relationship we have with our inner child may be tainted by our experiences. To truly be globally valuable in our own eyes, we need to be self-accepted. Self-esteem doesn't have quite the right vigor. Self-esteem is how we value our worth and how confident we feel in life, but it doesn't mean we don't falter at the sight of weakness. Self-esteem is the perception of having no flaws, but that's a lie. Self-acceptance is an unconditional concept. It means we're able to completely accept every facet of our beings, including our strengths and weaknesses. It means we can embrace whatever comes, even if it's not positive or worthy of an Oscar. Self-acceptance allows us to recognize our vulnerabilities, limitations, and weaknesses, but we don't berate ourselves for these flaws. We understand that perfection is a myth, and we don't allow imperfections to interfere with our acceptance.

Self-acceptance means you need to appreciate the fact that you're not responsible for your weaknesses. You're not to blame for anything, not even your genetics, subjective attractiveness, intelligence, or behaviors. Even your questionable behaviors are not always the product of your making. They're regulated by a combination of your biology and experience, but every flaw makes your authentic self more beautiful and unique. Just as your perceptions of the world have been designed by your childhood, so has your ability to love and appreciate yourself. You only accept yourself the same way your parents, teachers, and friends did. Your ability to appreciate yourself is already conditioned by age eight (Seltzer, 2011). Your behaviors are erratic and irrational before this.

The way your parents choose to love you unconditionally, or the way they punish or encourage you, can change the way you love yourself. Parents who focus on everything their toddlers do wrong are likely to instill a lack of self-appreciation, but parents who motivate their toddlers and praise them will instill self-love. Parents who never separated you from your erratic behavior as an independent child were not teaching you to appreciate yourself. A child and their behaviors are separate entities, and anyone who places them in the same pot is teaching the child that their behaviors define their character. If the behavior is unacceptable, so is the child. The more objectionable we see our behaviors, the more likely we are to consider ourselves inadequate. Almost every adult thinks they're inadequate to some degree.

Removing the conditions for which you appreciate, accept, and love yourself helps you reduce the self-doubt that stands in the way of a better relationship with your inner self. Beating yourself up for a mistake means you love yourself conditionally. Moving forward from the mistake and accepting your stumble as a once-off incident can help you restore unconditional love for yourself. You're not defective or to blame for everything wrong in the world. You must learn to accept every part of yourself, even the shadow self. The shadow self is one that has questionable thoughts, such as wanting to punch someone in the face. Your shadow self can be as dark as wanting to hurt someone, or it can be as child-like as wanting to throw eggs at someone's car. The shadow self creates fantasies.

For you to accept yourself completely, you need to show love and compassion for each self inside of you, including the inner critic. Accepting them doesn't mean you allow the shadow self to act on its whims, but you must accept that it's a part of you. It's an imperfection, and in all honesty, there's nothing more beautiful than imperfection. Self-compassion is a gateway to your self-acceptance. It means you can't judge yourself for the thoughts you possess, whether they're positive or negative. You can't judge yourself for the way you were raised, but you can change the here and now. That's the secret with self-compassion. It's a present concept. You can't be self-compassionate with the past or future, but you can accept yourself today. Self-compassion is void of evaluating your worthiness in this world.

Self-compassion is a kind way in which you relate to your achievements, shortfalls, and yourself. You'll learn to accept yourself with all your imperfections and inadequacies, both of which are limited to perception anyway. Self-compassion is a way to enhance your happiness, life satisfaction, emotional intelligence, resilience, and well-being, according to clinical social worker Allison Abrams (Abrams & Schrader, 2017). Self-compassion also reduces shame, depression, anxiety, and the fear of failure. Accepting yourself and practicing self-compassion strengthens your mind because you won't be seeking validation from others. You'll have a better self-concept, reduced narcissism, decreased reactivity in thought and behavior, and you'll have better relationships. There are a few ways in which you can cultivate self-compassion.

Imagine yourself as a child, and consider how you can be more compassionate to this small person to make their future brighter and happier. How would you treat a child who has come through a painful or stressful situation? Children are delicate, and you know how impressionable they can be now, so consider how you'd raise this inner child differently from how you were raised.

Remember that you're also not alone in this world. Shared humanity is a genuine concept of which you can remind yourself. You're imperfect in some ways, but so is everyone else. You're a part of a larger entity that drives the evolution of mankind. Appreciate that other people also experience trials and negative situations, and know that every human has their limits. Every person needs to forgive themselves, or evolution will halt as mankind cannot move past their faults. Recognize your shared humanity, and you'll feel much closer and happier with all the other imperfect people in this world. The human condition is imperfect, so don't expect yourself to be what is biologically impossible.

Permit yourself to be human with all your flaws and greatness combined. You're allowed to be unproductive from time to time. It's okay to feel like the day has gone wrong. It's also okay to hole up in your apartment over the weekend to recover from a setback, but the trick is to allow yourself to feel the way you do without letting it define your entire future. Permitting yourself to be imperfect is a way to change your perspective of yourself.

Releasing statements can also help you find compassion when your inner critic is telling you to beat yourself up. Release yourself from negative emotions and thoughts by accepting them. Releasing statements are self-forgiveness. When your inner critic says you should be ashamed of the way you behaved, reply to it by saying, "It's okay to feel ashamed because I'm only human." When it says, "You're stupid for not being able to solve the problem," You can say, "It's okay not to solve the problem on my first try. I need to learn something new to resolve it now." You're permitting yourself to forgive the minor setback without defining your entire being when you use releasing statements.

You can also see a therapist if you find it difficult to embrace self-compassion. A supportive therapist or coach can help you recognize your emotions and thoughts. They can share realistic perspectives and show you empathy. An empathetic coach can guide you back to your authentic self by teaching you how to accept your truth.

Self-compassion is the first step to accepting yourself as imperfectly amazing. You also need to practice self-care and self-love to reinforce your self-acceptance.

Much Needed Care

Failing to care for yourself leaves a door open to self-defeating and negative thoughts and emotions. Feeling uncomfortable in your own skin makes your inner selves feel less worthy than they should. Your internal and external environments should be looked after. You automatically feel and think better when you have a nice meal, dress warm, and get enough rest. Your basic human needs must be cared for to make a difference in your self-acceptance. Does your friend feel more appreciated and accepted when you actionably care about their needs, or is it acceptable to just say it? Care for your mind like a loved one, and you'll be on your way to an optimistic attitude.

According to Harvard Medical School, you can keep your mind healthy, strong, positive, and young by stimulating your brain (Harvard Health Publishing, 2018). Stimulating your brain with exercises can forge new connections between various regions, improving your focus, memory, and concentration. Ways to stimulate it include crossword puzzles, reading a book, math or memory games, and learning a new skill like a musical instrument. Keeping your mind healthy is an essential part of self-care.

Challenging yourself also encourages the brain to work harder, which has the same benefits as mental stimulation exercises. Challenge your brain creatively or intellectually. Sometimes, the two are one of the same. Learn a new word each day or a language you always found intriguing. Take art classes to improve your painting skills, or try a new hobby that may ignite an innate talent. Try a new recipe, or look for inspiration where you never thought possible. Challenging yourself is fun and a way of caring for your brain.

The body carries the mind, and caring about your physical health is self-care. It's common knowledge that exercise releases feel-good hormones like dopamine and serotonin. Your mental, emotional, and physical well-being changes as you exercise. Cardiovascular workouts also improve your blood flow, allowing the brain and other vital organs to receive oxygen-rich blood. The neurons and prefrontal cortex receive better oxygen, which enhances your focus, rationale, and memory. Exercise also decreases your risk of cognitive decline, which is responsible for dementia. Walking, cycling, or swimming for half an hour daily does the trick. Exercise for five days and rest for two every week.

A mental cleanse is another necessity for self-care. We must dump our limiting beliefs, negative thinking patterns, and unwanted habits to give the mind enough space to flourish. Journaling is a brain-dumping method you can use to release your thoughts and emotions, but you can also commit to practicing better habits daily to see changes in your attitude. Focus on what you can control, and allow yourself to embrace negative feelings without judgment.

A digital detox is another way to declutter the mind for improved well-being. This isn't the same as toning down your media usage. You want to reduce your technology usage as well. Switch your phone off, and read a book instead of watching Netflix. Technology can be counterproductive to the brain. It distracts your mind from things that matter more. Give yourself time to recuperate from the digital world for an hour, and when you remember how incredible the world is beyond technology, you can increase your detox times until you reach 24 hours at a time.

Being silent and alone with your thoughts and emotions can be intimidating, but it's another way to practice mental self-care. The problem is that avoiding thoughts only makes them return. You have to embrace the stillness that allows your thoughts to be part of your inner self, and you can do this with meditation. Meditation allows time to be silent and to recognize the thoughts that run amok. Mindfulness meditation works well.

Self-care for the mind means you need to pause from time to time. Take a mental health day, or a few hours weekly if you can't afford an entire day, and just practice one or more of the mental self-care tips. Meditate, do a crossword, be still, or just go for a walk. Turn your electronics off during this time to be with your mind and inner selves.

A healthier mind leads to less resistance to self-acceptance, so it's an essential part of your journey to an optimistic attitude. Caring for yourself also gives you the energy to face negative patterns without succumbing to them.

Nutrition for the Self

Your inner selves need nutrition, and self-love can provide just that. Think of the inner critic who acts like a child. Children often become erratic when they're hungry. The shadow self also needs nutrition, or it will find ways to be louder. The authentic self needs the most nutrition because it wasn't the strongest until now. Nutrition ignites the growth of your inner truth, and this helps you accept yourself and be more optimistic. Think of self-love as the fuel that fills your self-acceptance tank. There are ways to acceptably love yourself more.

Forgiving yourself must be the hardest thing you can do, but it's an act of self-love. Ask yourself with sincere honesty if there's something you need to forgive yourself for. Chances are that you've said or done something to yourself or others you regret. A slip of the tongue or an inconsiderate decision is something we all do, and it's often ignited by the shadow self or the demon-child. Take a moment to ponder on what you regret, and then you can write it down on paper. Read it back to yourself aloud, and you'll quickly realize that you don't need to feel the burden anymore.

Keep a to-do list for things that inspire you. You want to be more optimistic, so add mind-changing practices to a daily list. Don't beat yourself up for skipping one or two, either. You should love yourself, irrespective of mishaps along the way. Your list may include getting more sleep, working out, reframing your thoughts, or attending a conference about positive mindsets. Add whatever makes you feel good because you want to inspire better satisfaction with your present self.

Reframe your self-concept by thinking about what you haven't loved about yourself before. What new part of you can you love today, one that hasn't been loved before? Perhaps you don't love your physical persona. Choose to love something about it today. You can say, "My arms might be long, but that makes it easier for me to reach higher places. My legs may be scrawny, but they allow me to buy any shape of boot." Reframe what you didn't love before to make you appreciate it in a new light.

Loving yourself also means you're prepared to take action against anything that negatively affects you. If you have negative friends, get new ones. If your work environment is negative, start shopping for new employment. If your partner only undermines your every thought, you may be limited in business. Get rid of that which hinders your forward momentum. Surround yourself with elements and people that push you forward.

Self-love also requires you to fill the tanks of your physical, emotional, mental, and spiritual needs as a human. Stick to healthier lifestyles by cutting out cigarettes, alcohol, and any substance that affects your thoughts. Practice techniques that improve your emotional and mental well-being. What people fail to realize is that spiritualism is also a love for themselves. They love themselves enough to accept responsibility for their minor contributions to a scheme greater than themselves. All aspects of health link back to self care.

Love yourself enough to know when you need comfort, soothing, or validation. Your emotions are relevant, and you're allowed to validate them. Always remember that you're only human, and your emotions are as relevant as the seasons. It's okay to feel bad once in a while. Life isn't joyful or perfect every day. Take time to be still with yourself, and comfort yourself for the changing tides that life tends to bring. Just remember that calmness always follows a crashing wave. Don't ruminate. Rather linger on the positive times and memories.

Self-love can be as simple as reading books. A review published in the *Proceedings of the National Academy of Sciences* explains that reading can reduce stress, help you sleep better, and stave off Alzheimer's disease (Friedland et al., 2001). Reading is a way to sharpen your mind, which improves your overall well-being, making it another act of self-love. Love yourself enough to read books that challenge you and make you feel happier about yourself. Read real books and not the kind that glimmers behind a screen.

Start building daily habits with specific behaviors you want to practice. This also shows an increased love for yourself because you value yourself enough to turn negative thoughts into positive ones. Your daily routine should combine self-care, self-compassion, and self-love, and it should include a few ways you can change your mind to reflect your authentic self. Then, you can repeat the habits that slowly start making you learn to accept your inner truths.

One secret you must know is that not all happiness is equally designed, either. Pleasure, joy, and bliss are short-lived, but meaningful happiness is a long-term source. Seeking meaning over pleasure leads to eudaimonic happiness, which is the kind you build over a lifetime. It's the kind you look back on and feel a sense of pride and accomplishment. It's when you reminisce on the meaningful and good quality of life you lived. It's where you don't regret your decisions because you forgave your mistakes. Meaningful pursuits are when you seek a purpose in life. It's not about getting the next fix of pleasure.

Loving yourself for who you are and all your imperfections can help you accept the authentic part of yourself. This paves the way to a better quality of life and optimism. All you need now is to recognize how much control you possess.

Chapter 7:

You're in Control

All this talk about what can and can't be controlled certainly brews doubt, but it needs to be said again, you can control your thoughts, irrespective of your experiences. Indeed, your experiences have either made it simpler or more complicated, but it can be done. You have more control over your thoughts than you think. It's simply a matter of practice.

Mind Your Control

Your mind is a map to something greater, a treasure if you must, and some famous people have found the treasure in mastering their minds. All of the great people we know today have overcome some form of fear that would've prevented them from being known if they didn't see the silver lining of possibility. Abraham Lincoln could only have been frightened by the potential dangers he faced from many of his own people when he ended slavery. However, he still managed to push ahead. Gautama Buddha who we're learning to know in the West was not always a thinker.

He started as a prince who chose to leave royalty behind so he could embrace something greater, and look at what happened to him.

Jesus can also be considered here. He had many fears, and his life was hanging by a thread as he walked into the most dangerous civilizations. Yet, his name is still known today. What about Neil Armstrong? Imagine how many questions ran through his mind before he set foot on the moon. What if he fails? What if the worst happens? Well, if Armstrong gave in to his fears, the American flag might never have made it to the moon first. When we question ourselves and our abilities to master our thoughts and fears, we begin establishing something great. We become capable of controlling what happens in our minds. Ask yourself if your mental map should lead you to a treasure of an unknown but fruitful kind, or do you want to lose the opportunities that may exist?

Controlling your thoughts isn't only possible; it's also how you become your greatest self. You still accept yourself in every present moment, but you'll look back one day and realize that your life was well worth living. Your mind can be your greatest asset or your worst enemy, and the result is your choice. If you want an asset that brings you closer to your dreams, you must take control of the way you think. Your thoughts can destroy the beauty and strength of your mind, so consider whether you want to destroy the control you have. Too many people don't allow intentions to guide their thoughts. They accumulate all kinds of thoughts until their minds erupt with damaging results. They don't prioritize what they must think about. You have to control and protect your mind from what you don't desire.

When you control your thoughts, you can influence the direction of your life, well-being, and success. The source of your fears is your mind, so controlling your mind is like mastering your fears. You can discipline your mind enough to focus on noble, positive, and admirable thinking. People will still challenge your mind and instill new fears, but having control over your mind reduces the impact. You'll have to make some sacrifices, and the journey will be hard, but you'll find freedom when you master your mind with grit and consistency. Mastering your mind is about choosing to use conscious thoughts. You must be aware of your thinking, and then you can change it.

With time, your changed thoughts also reduce the impact of the related feelings, allowing you to decrease the triggers that once made you negative.

Mastering Your Mind

To grab the face of fear and irrational expectations by the horns, you must gain a level of mastery. Don't expect yourself to master your mind overnight because that would mean you're not caring about yourself. You won't be self-accepting if you think you should master your mind instantaneously. Remember that self-acceptance must be in the present, and your dreams and hopes for a better, healthier, happier, and more positive future lie ahead of you. Consciously thinking about what potentially lies ahead can also boost your acceptance here and now. A few techniques can help you master your thinking.

Consider every experience you pursue as nutrition for your mind. Feeding your body nutritious food sustains better well-being, so feeding the mind with the right words and images does the same. Only nourish your mind with images and words that promote optimism. Stop watching television that makes you feel frustrated, and delete social media friends and pages who share negative content. Reconsider the dinner with friends if all they can do is undermine someone behind their backs. Any form of negative persuasion can change your ability to control your thoughts. Consuming even the smallest negativities intentionally is like drinking poison and expecting to be safe.

Use affirmations to enhance your positive control over your thoughts. Affirmations remind you to master your mind, and it helps to have a few ready to alternate between every hour. You can also add sticky notes to your home, car, and office. These notes help you keep track of your thoughts when they stray during common trigger situations, too. Having a note in the office that simply reads "I can do this" or "I'm willing to do my best" can counter the negative thoughts at work. Use your thought diary to write personal affirmations that counter the common thoughts you want to control, and you can write a few positive quotes or sayings to inspire you.

One benefit you have of choosing to focus on your thoughts consciously is that you also start seeing which thoughts need to be trashed. Often, old thoughts and beliefs have a way of sneaking into our minds when we think we forgot about them. Having a keener sense of awareness prevents these thoughts from surprising you, and you can work on throwing them out. Thoughts that don't serve you in a positive light need to be replaced, and you can do this by acknowledging some of them long enough for self-removal. Otherwise, you can prove them wrong by replacing them with a realistic and positive alternative. Your thoughts must serve you in some way, and any pattern that doesn't move you closer to your dreams should be substituted with one that does. Use meditation to surface these thoughts.

Controlling your mind also means you should establish a personal mental stop sign. You can go with the classic of imagining a stop sign when you consciously notice negative thinking, or you can design a unique one that suits you better. You may choose to imagine a hand while you mentally tell your inner critic to be quiet. You can tell them to stop in your mind because you have the power to do so. Stop signs take practice and time to establish, but you'll have better control over your inner thoughts when you establish one you can use anywhere. It doesn't matter what your stop sign looks or sounds like. It must be ready for use whenever you feel a negative thought sliding into your mind. This sudden assertiveness over your thoughts brings you back to the present moment and away from past or future thoughts.

Your body has two ways of alerting you that your thoughts are running wild again. The emotional guidance system is your first warning. You must befriend your emotional guidance system to be aware of the changes and take action quickly. Your emotions can indicate that you're on your best path or you've steered far away from it. You have to be mindful of your emotions as much as possible, and this may help you stop your thoughts from running away before your behavior changes. You don't want your emotions to automatically be influenced by your previous beliefs or pessimism. Every time you experience an emotion, whether it's utter rage, mere frustration, anxiety, or a boost of adrenaline, listen to your thoughts before they progress your mindset further down the well. Evaluate your thoughts before any momentum exists. This is how you help yourself release emotions before your mind reacts to them.

The second way your body alerts you of negative thinking is when your emotions have broken into a physical reaction. You may feel a knot in your stomach, a sudden and unexplainable headache, or your palms could become sweaty. Your heart might race, and your forehead might turn damp with sweat. This results from the stress response ignited by your emotions and thoughts. Even the beginning of the common cold may indicate that you need to pay attention to your thoughts because your thinking patterns could make your immune system weaker. Don't be afraid of this natural process though. This is the second way your emotional guidance system is trying to grab your attention. It means you need to listen to your thoughts and reevaluate them before it gets worse. Your biology is the best guidance system to encourage you to change direction.

Step-by-Step Control

Being in control of your mind can open your life to new opportunities and leave old habits behind. Four steps can bring you closer to control if you practice them daily.

Step one is to recognize which thoughts you'd like to change. You must learn to know your mind before you control it. The cognitive distortions show you patterns within your thoughts, but a few other vagrants live inside your head. The authentic self, shadow self, and inner critic are three of the vagrants, but there are more. Knowing their names and intentions could help you to identify them.

The inner critic is the one that keeps making you doubt yourself. He's the one that abuses you with other people's words and comparisons. He also instigates thoughts based on other people's expectations. Feelings of rejection and betrayal also come from the inner critic. He's all about low self-esteem, suffering, and a lack of self-acceptance.

The worrier self is the future-dated one that makes you think "what if?" Fear drives the worrier, and he has no logic. The worrier fears the future because he thinks things will always happen as they did before.

The reactor self is the one that deals anger, frustration, and disappointment cards. He lives in the past, and he's triggered by anything that reminds you of trauma or unpleasantry you experienced before.

Then comes the sleep depriver, who is also made of the ruminator, rehasher, and planner. He is the head of this committee, and he hates silence. He wants to revisit all the things you missed today, and he intends to boost the inner critic's voice.

The inner critic and the worrier are best addressed by replacing the thoughts you experience, but the reactor and sleep deprivation committee should be silenced as much as possible. Identify which voices are speaking up after you recognized your cognitive distortion, and then address them as you need to. Your control over the inner critic and worrier is your best bet, and controlling them will automatically start silencing the reactor and the insomnia committee.

Step two is to accept the unwanted thoughts as counterproductive. These thoughts belong to you, and you can't avoid them. Pushing them away will only intensify them, so you must embrace your inner voices, even the reactor, and the sleep depriver. Acceptance of your thoughts is part of self-acceptance, and it will help you control them. Let's say you're feeling down because your life isn't going as well as you planned. You won't focus on the sleep depriver to control this. You'd focus on the inner critic that fuels the sleep depriver.

First, accept the relevancy of the thought. You can tell yourself, "I know life isn't going as I planned right now, and that's disappointing, but I can only do so much to move forward at once. Giving up isn't the answer. I need to rethink my strategy at the time I've allocated to it in my daily planner." Notice how you dedicate specific time to focus on the new plan. This eases the sleep depriver when he knows you'll be working on it. Second, you should be addressing the plan, which comes in step three.

Step three is where you define your future self. You redefine the habits of who you want to be, where your life must head, and what you want to think. You'll have to create new habits and routines that help you become the person you desire, and they help you achieve the direction you want to see in your life. Having a plan to change your habits is a simpler way to hush the inner critic and worrier, allowing your reactor and sleep depriver to remain dormant. You'll have better and consistent control over your thoughts. First, ask yourself how you want to think from now. Do you want to stop worrying so much? Do you want to feel stressed, or would you like to be in control?

Take a moment to imagine yourself thinking the way you want to. How would you feel if you thought this way? If you can find the willpower to tell your inner selves that you don't want to think a certain way anymore, you're already stronger than you think. That's only the first part of your plan. The second part of the plan is to imagine the person you dream of becoming. Envisioning yourself has a great influence over what you achieve. Monks spend years or even lifetimes meditating. They're training their minds to be still and visualize greater things. You don't have to be a monk, but visualizing your planned self can have a huge impact on your mind. Anyway, envision yourself being confident if you lack it. Imagine yourself being a social butterfly if you struggle with dating.

Imagine yourself completing a presentation if you feel anxious each time you start one. Maybe you plan to become a calmer, more zen person. Perhaps you wish to be mindful. Write this down on your plan, and envision yourself in this outcome repeatedly. Don't just imagine yourself standing on a stage after overcoming your fear of public speaking. Imagine your new self from the time you wake up to the time you rest your head at night. Imagine what you'll eat for breakfast and which clothes you'll wear to boost your professionalism at work. Imagine your mind feeling clear and motivated in the morning. Envision yourself dealing with traffic by listening to a great self-improvement audiobook. Imagine yourself handling confrontation better at work, the supermarket, or when you get home.

Moreover, visualize yourself disconnecting from the long day of work when you get home. Your visualization plans should be elaborately detailed, and you should spend at least 20 minutes daily inside this future plan. The mind will watch, and the inner voices will pay attention to the way this vision makes you feel. Planning your new habits and routines in this way will condition the mind to better accept the new strategy with repeated practice. This plan also gives you ideas of how to react to people without waking the reactor when someone upsets you. It also starts igniting motivation when you feel the pressure to start a new project. Convince your mind you're in control, and it will become true. By conditioning the mind this way, you're designing a map that easily shows it exactly how you want to be.

Step four is to tap into your deepest desires. Convincing your mind to follow the new plan won't be easy, but it's a simpler change if you follow your desires. Nothing worthwhile in this world has ever come easy, so changing your habits won't, either. Armstrong was afraid, and so were Buddha, Jesus, and Lincoln. The difference with these successful giants is that they persevered by following a passion. If you desire something enough, it will come to fruition. You simply have to stay the course. Spend 10 minutes every morning grounding yourself in your calmer and more positive mindset. Breathe in deeply, and allow the air to flow through your deepest parts. Address negative self-talk as it happens throughout the day because there will be resistance, even if you desire something. Then, rehearse your plan every night for 20 minutes.

The Toolkit

If you need tools to help you stay the course of your plan, you can use the toolkit that abruptly stops the inner voices in their tracks. This actionable toolkit pulls you out of a negative state by activating changes in your brain.

First, force a smile. Forcing a smile is a controlled muscle traction, which tells the brain that you're feeling better. Even a fake smile works.

Second, propel your arms into the air like you're about to ride a rollercoaster. This is another forced muscle traction that disrupts the train of thought in your mind. Your mind listens to your body, so use this as an advantage. Physical motion ignites emotions, which affect your thoughts. Also, you'll get your blood pumping.

Third, repeat a personal mantra or affirmation you designed. Vocalize your mantra. It can be as simple as "I've got this" or "I'm amped for this!" Speaking out loud also stops the train of thought.

Fourth, exhale deeply and imagine the tension in your body leaving as the air flows out. Let go of the thoughts by releasing them, and feel yourself relax. Repeat your deep exhales as many times as you have to throughout the day.

Each tool can be used individually, too. Embrace your changing habits, and use the toolkit to disrupt negative thoughts before they convince your mind that your plan isn't working. You're in control, not your thoughts. Own them, and condition them to be what you design.

Conclusion

Will your mind be a threat to your quality of life, or will you use it to inspire and ignite the best life you can live? That's entirely up to you now. Being negative has too many consequences and setbacks. It can strip you of your joy, and it can steal your mental health in a matter of seconds. The response of your brain to your mind is incredibly powerful, and pessimism doesn't make this relationship any better. You need to consider how often you want to be stuck in the negative cycle again. There's nothing worthwhile in this mindset. It only beats you up and leaves you for the dogs. Negativity turns you into a person with no self-esteem or confidence, and your days are filled with insecurities. You become restrained in everything you desire, whether it's success, love, happiness, or peak health.

Pessimism holds you back from the life you can have. It takes away the moments you can cherish, and it reduces your ability to cope with the moments you wish to overcome. It can even make you feel helpless, and you won't know where to turn, whom to speak to, or what to do next. Suddenly, you have all these thoughts that only make you feel worse. You'll never be good, intelligent, or attractive enough to meet the standards set within your mind. You'll always compare yourself to plastic fallacies that don't exist. You won't make the best of your life if you're always allowing others to guide your thoughts. You'll always doubt everything and everyone, including yourself. This doubt will bubble in your mind until you're not sure you can change it anymore, but that's not true. You can always change. Negativity just doesn't allow you to believe this.

Again, do you want to become the master of your thoughts, or do you want them to unravel dangerous and unproductive situations in your life? There's no need for you to believe you can't change anymore. You know how your thoughts work now. You know how the human mind can impact every part of your being and health. You know what happens to your brain and your body when it goes unmanaged, so you won't be leaving your thoughts to do their thing anymore. You also learned about where your thoughts came from, and how the domino effect starts under your conscious awareness. No one desires the potential risks involved with being a pessimist. Everyone desires the best life they can live, and you're no different. Your mind stood in your way before, but you can start changing that.

It won't change overnight, and it certainly won't happen by wearing rose-colored glasses when life doesn't always play fair. It happens with conscious effort, practice, and time. Remember why your thoughts can't just be changed. Keep in mind the reasons your mind and brain will retaliate against a sudden and mismanaged change. Once you realize how your mindset must be shifted, you can start recognizing the thoughts that plague you. There are more than 20 types of thoughts that could damage your quality of life. Who knew there were so many? Some of them are subtler, so be careful to really listen to your thoughts. Embrace your feelings and behaviors to understand them better, too. Once identified, you can start taking back control of the doubters, critics, and demons inside your mind.

Some negative thoughts might serve a purpose, but many of the untruths spoken by these demons can make you miss opportunities to succeed in the ways you desire. You can't allow them to run amok while you try to clean up after them. After silencing the inner voices that amplify unjust thoughts, you can assert a protective layer in your mind with simple practices and techniques that encourage resilience and authenticity. You can start awakening the inner selves that motivate and improve your journey through this world. Moreover, you'll strengthen your relationships with the right thoughts when you practice your self-acceptance and self-care. This is a relationship that further amplifies the protection of your mind. You have basic needs just like anyone else, and your mind has basic needs of its own.

Stop watering a plant and see what happens. It doesn't flourish. It withers until nothing remains. Your mind is like a plant that needs nourishment, and your conscious mind can provide it. The fallacy of control is only relevant to what you can't control. You can control and manage your thoughts through mental discipline and step-by-step practice. If all else fails, you have the four tools that can change your mind within seconds to stop a train of thought that doesn't serve you. Your desired changes and mastery are in your hands now, and you can always seek professional help if you're coming against roadblocks you can't overcome. This book has been based on scientific evidence of what happens in the human mind. I only rely on evidence to support my books, but I also throw a splash of passion into them because I can relate to your trials.

I also stood on this crossroad a few years ago, and I'm ecstatic that I chose the path I did. I chose to gradually change my thoughts. I became the master of my mind, and that allowed me to change the results in my life. I hope you find the same results, and you're welcome to review or comment on this book to let me know how my advice worked for you. I love speaking to the people I touch. My final words for you would be that you embrace the changes you can control because your mind is one of them.

References

Abrams, A., & Schrader, J. (2017, March 3). *How to cultivate more self-compassion.* Psychology Today. https://www.psychologytoday.com/us/blog/nurturing-self-compassion/201703/how-cultivate-more-self-compassion

Alliant International University. (2019). *How environmental factors impact mental health.* Alliant International University. https://www.alliant.edu/blog/how-environmental-factors-impact-mental-health

Anderson, J. (2014, June 12). *5 get-positive techniques from cognitive behavioral therapy.* Everyday Health. https://www.everydayhealth.com/hs/major-depression-living-well/cognitive-behavioral-therapy-techniques/

Best Brain Possible. (2018, July 22). *10 common negative thinking patterns and how you can change them.* The Best Brain Possible. https://thebestbrainpossible.com/negative-thinking-depression-mind/

Blades, G. (2017, March 6). *How to take control of your thoughts.* Geoff Blades.

https://geoffblades.com/take-control-thoughts/

Bonner, K. (2018, December 26). *What causes negative thinking & how to stop it*. Baptist Health Blog. https://share.baptisthealth.com/negative-thinking-patterns/

Brown, J., & Wong, J. (2017, June 6). *How gratitude changes you and your brain*. Greater Good. https://greatergood.berkeley.edu/article/item/how_gratitude_changes_you_and_your_brain

Cherry, K., & Swaim, E. (2020, April 29). *Why our brains are hardwired to focus on the negative*. Verywell Mind. https://www.verywellmind.com/negative-bias-4589618

Cicetti, F. (2013, May 30). *Can negative thoughts be stopped?* Live Science. https://www.livescience.com/36586-stop-negative-thoughts-depression.html

Colier, N. (2019, April 15). *Negative thinking: A dangerous addiction*. Psychology Today. https://www.psychologytoday.com/us/blog/inviting-monkey-tea/201904/negative-thinking-dangerous-addiction

Cuncic, A., & Morin, A. (2020, June 29). *How to change your negative thought patterns when you have SAD*. Verywell Mind.

https://www.verywellmind.com/how-to-change-negative-thinking-3024843

Dent Neurologic Institute. (2019, July 22). *22 facts about the brain | World Brain Day*. Dent Neurologic Institute. https://www.dentinstitute.com/posts/lifestyle-tips/22-facts-about-the-brain-world-brain-day/

Djordjevic, M. (2021, March 29). *17 undeniable negative news statistics you need to know*. Letter.ly. https://letter.ly/negative-news-statistics/

Elmer, J., & Legg, T. J. (2018, November 29). *Automatic negative thinking: 5 ways to stop these invading thoughts*. Healthline. https://www.healthline.com/health/mental-health/stop-automatic-negative-thoughts#2-recognize-automatic-negative-thinking

Everson-Rose, S. A., Roetker, N. S., Lutsey, P. L., Kershaw, K., Longstreth, W., Sacco, R. L., Roux, A. V. D., & Alonso, A. (2014). Chronic stress, depressive symptoms, anger, hostility and risk of stroke and transient ischemic attack in the MESA study. *Stroke; a Journal of Cerebral Circulation*, *45*(8), 2318–2323. https://doi.org/10.1161/STROKEAHA.114.004815

Exploring Your Mind. (2019, April 23). *Learn to identify automatic negative thoughts*. Exploring Your Mind.

https://exploringyourmind.com/learn-to-identify-automatic-negative-thoughts/

Firestone, L. (2014, August 20). *How negative thoughts are ruining your life.* Psychology Today. https://www.psychologytoday.com/us/blog/compassion-matters/201408/how-negative-thoughts-are-ruining-your-life

Friedland, R. P., Fritsch, T., Smyth, K. A., Koss, E., Lerner, A. J., Chen, C. H., Petot, G. J., & Debanne, S. M. (2001). Patients with Alzheimer's disease have reduced activities in midlife compared with healthy control-group members. *Proceedings of the National Academy of Sciences, 98*(6), 3440–3445. https://doi.org/10.1073/pnas.061002998

Gayathri Rao. (2016, September 13). *What are negative thoughts?* Your Dost Blog. https://yourdost.com/blog/2016/09/what-are-negative-thoughts.html?q=/blog/2016/09/what-are-negative-thoughts.html&q=/blog/2016/09/what-are-negative-thoughts.html&

Goldstein, M. (2013, April 20). *How to control your thoughts and be the master of your mind.* Lifehack. https://www.lifehack.org/articles/lifestyle/how-to-master-your-mind-part-one-whos-running-your-thoughts.html

Gregoire, C. (2013, November 8). *9 ways to become the master of your own mind.* HuffPost. https://www.huffpost.com/entry/master-your-mind_n_4214783

Harvard Health Publishing. (2018, January 16). *12 ways to keep your brain young.* Harvard Health; https://www.health.harvard.edu/mind-and-mood/12-ways-to-keep-your-brain-young

Hoffman, A. (2015, June 26). *Can negative thinking make you sick?* Health. https://www.health.com/condition/heart-disease/can-negative-thinking-make-you-sick

Holmes, J. C. (2015, February 18). *The root of negative thinking.* Janae's Blog. https://janaecookieholmes.weebly.com/blog/the-root-of-negative-thinking

Kinderman, P., Schwannauer, M., Pontin, E., & Tai, S. (2013). Psychological processes mediate the impact of familial risk, social circumstances and life events on mental health. *PLoS ONE, 8*(10), e76564. https://doi.org/10.1371/journal.pone.0076564

Lawson, K. (2012). *How do thoughts and emotions affect health?* University of Minnesota. https://www.takingcharge.csh.umn.edu/how-do-thoughts-and-emotions-affect-health

Maloney, B. (2018, January 18). *The damaging effects of negativity*. Marque Medical. https://marquemedical.com/damaging-effects-of-negativity/

Marchant, N. L., Lovland, L. R., Jones, R., Pichet Binette, A., Gonneaud, J., Arenaza-Urquijo, E. M., Chételat, G., & Villeneuve, S. (2020). Repetitive negative thinking is associated with amyloid, tau, and cognitive decline. *Alzheimer's & Dementia, 16*(7). https://doi.org/10.1002/alz.12116

Marteka. (2019, July 15). 12 ways to recognise negative thoughts. Benevolent Health. https://benevolenthealth.co.uk/12-ways-to-recognise-negative-thoughts/

Mohammadkhani, P., Bagheri, M., Dobson, K. S., Eskandari, E., Dejman, M., Bass, J., & Abdi, F. (2018). Negative thoughts in depression: A study in Iran. *International Journal of Psychology*. https://doi.org/10.1002/ijop.12541

Moore, C. (2019, June 2). *How to practice self-compassion: 8 techniques and tips*. Positive Psychology. https://positivepsychology.com/how-to-practice-self-compassion/

O'Brien, M. (2018, August 20). *4 keys to overcoming negative thinking for good*. Mrs. Mindfulness. https://mrsmindfulness.com/the-four-keys-to-overcoming-negative-thinkingfor-good/

O'Donovan, K. (2013, November 26). *10 negative thoughts we all have and what we should think instead.* Lifehack. https://www.lifehack.org/articles/communication/10-negative-thoughts-all-have-and-what-should-think-instead.html

Pastiloff, J. (2011, November 2). *Love yourself, accept yourself, forgive yourself.* Tiny Buddha. https://tinybuddha.com/blog/love-yourself-accept-yourself-forgive-yourself/

Paul, M. (2006, December 31). *Are you addicted to negative thinking?* Inner Bonding. https://www.innerbonding.com/show-article/809/are-you-addicted-to-negative-thinking.html

Paula. (2020, January 31). *9 self-care practices for the mind.* Thirteen Thoughts. https://www.thirteenthoughts.com/self-care-practices-for-the-mind/

Pavlok. (2017). *The damaging effects of negative thoughts (and how to stop them with Pavlok).* Pavlok. https://pavlok.com/damaging-effects-negative-thoughts-stop-pavlok/

Pratt, E., & Gifford, M. (2020, June 11). *Negative thinking can harm your brain and increase your dementia risk.* Healthline. https://www.healthline.com/health-news/negative-thinking-can-harm-brain-increase-dementia-risk

Querstret, D., & Cropley, M. (2013). Assessing treatments used to reduce rumination and/or worry: A systematic review. *Clinical Psychology Review*, *33*(8), 996–1009. https://doi.org/10.1016/j.cpr.2013.08.004

Rajpal, D. (2014, May 11). *Guard your mind against the negative thoughts*. Success Consciousness. https://www.successconsciousness.com/blog/positive-attitude/guard-your-mind-against-the-negative-thoughts/

Raypole, C., & Legg, T. J. (2021, January 8). *How to control your mind: 10 techniques*. Healthline. https://www.healthline.com/health/mental-health/how-to-control-your-mind

Reynolds, S., & Aubele, T. (2011, August 2). *Happy brain, happy life*. Psychology Today. https://www.psychologytoday.com/us/blog/prime-your-gray-cells/201108/happy-brain-happy-life

Sawyer, K. (2017, August 16). *How to identify automatic negative thoughts*. His Heart Foundation. https://hisheartfoundation.org/how-to-identify-automatic-negative-thoughts/

Scott, E., & Morin, A. (2018). *How to reduce negative self-talk for a better life*. Verywell Mind.

https://www.verywellmind.com/negative-self-talk-and-how-it-affects-us-4161304

Seleni Institute. (2015, September 29). *7 ways to deal with negative thoughts.* Psychology Today. https://www.psychologytoday.com/us/blog/women-s-mental-health-matters/201509/7-ways-deal-negative-thoughts

Seltzer, L. F. (2011). *The path to unconditional self-acceptance.* Psychology Today. https://www.psychologytoday.com/us/blog/evolution-the-self/200809/the-path-unconditional-self-acceptance

Serio, C. D., & Romito, K. (2020, September 23). *Stop negative thoughts: Choosing a healthier way of thinking.* Mott Children. https://www.mottchildren.org/health-library/uf9857

Smith, E.-M., & Croft, H. (2019, June 19). *What is negative thinking? How it destroys your mental health.* Healthy Place. https://www.healthyplace.com/self-help/positivity/what-is-negative-thinking-how-it-destroys-your-mental-health

Souheli, M. (2019, January 15). *7 ways to cleanse your mind of negative thoughts.* Thrive Global. https://thriveglobal.com/stories/7-ways-to-cleanse-your-mind-of-negative-thoughts/

Stanborough, R. J., & Legg, T. J. (2020, February 4). *Cognitive restructuring: Techniques and examples.* Healthline. https://www.healthline.com/health/cognitive-restructuring

Tanjeloff, J. (2011, January 7). *Accepting & loving ourselves in 10 simple steps.* Tiny Buddha. https://tinybuddha.com/blog/accepting-loving-ourselves-in-10-steps/

Tindle, H. A., Chang, Y.-F., Kuller, L. H., Manson, J. E., Robinson, J. G., Rosal, M. C., Siegle, G. J., & Matthews, K. A. (2009). Optimism, cynical hostility, and incident coronary heart disease and mortality in the women's health initiative. *Circulation*, *120*(8), 656–662. https://doi.org/10.1161/circulationaha.108.827642

Tuncel, K. (2019, August 6). *Why do negative thoughts come to my mind?* Thrive Global. https://thriveglobal.com/stories/why-do-negative-thoughts-come-to-my-mind/

Uniacke, K. (2018, May 8). *8 easy ways to stop negative thoughts from entering your mind.* A Conscious Rethink. https://www.aconsciousrethink.com/7829/stop-negative-thoughts/

Wallenda, N. (2020, September 15). *Why you have to take control of your thoughts.* Success.

https://www.success.com/why-you-have-to-take-control-of-your-thoughts/

Wenzlaff, R. M., & Wegner, D. M. (2000). Thought suppression. *Annual Review of Psychology*, *51*(1), 59–91. https://doi.org/10.1146/annurev.psych.51.1.59

West, N. L. (2015, June 19). *7 ways to truly master your own mind.* Lifehack. https://www.lifehack.org/277303/7-ways-truly-control-your-own-mind

Wolff, C. (2019, March 18). *How negativity actually messes with your brain chemistry.* Fab Fit Fun. https://fabfitfun.com/magazine/negativity-effects-brain-chemistry/

Woolston, C. (2019, December 31). *Overcoming negative thinking.* Consumer Health News. https://consumer.healthday.com/encyclopedia/depression-12/depression-news-176/overcoming-negative-thinking-645055.html

www.ingramcontent.com/pod-product-compliance
Lightning Source LLC
Chambersburg PA
CBHW021440080526
44588CB00009B/615